Daisy Miller and *The Turn of the Screw* may be Henry James's most widely read tales. Certainly, these swiftly moving accounts of failed connections are among the best examples of his shorter fiction. One represents the international theme that made him famous; the other exemplifies the multiple meanings that make him modern. The introduction to this volume locates his fiction in the context of the family that conditioned his concern with the sexual politics of intimate experience. In the four essays that follow, Kenneth Graham offers a close reading of *Daisy* that emphasizes the heroine's unknowability; Robert Weisbuch examines Winterbourne as a specimen of James's formidable bachelor type; Millicent Bell places the ghost story governess in the traditions of English fiction and society; and David McWhirter provides a critique of female authority. Deftly summarizing earlier criticism, these essays demonstrate the continuing appeal of Henry James in our time.

NEW ESSAYS ON DAISY MILLER
AND THE TURN OF THE SCREW

★ The American Novel ★

GENERAL EDITOR
Emory Elliott
University of California, Riverside

New Essays on Daisy Miller
and The Turn of the Screw

Edited by
Vivian R. Pollak

CAMBRIDGE
UNIVERSITY PRESS

Published by the Press Syndicate of the University of Cambridge
The Pitt Building, Trumpington Street, Cambridge CB2 1RP
40 West 20th Street, New York, NY 10011–4211, USA
10 Stamford Road, Oakleigh, Victoria 3166, Australia

First published 1993

Printed in the United States of America

Library of Congress Cataloging-in-Publication Data

New essays on Daisy Miller and The turn of the screw / edited by
Vivian R. Pollak.
p.   cm. – (The American novel)
Includes bibliographical references.
ISBN 0-521-41673-6 (hardcover). – ISBN 0-521-42681-2 (pbk.)
1. James, Henry, 1843–1916. Daisy Miller.   2. James, Henry,
1843–1916.   Turn of the screw.   I. Pollak, Vivian R.   II. Series.
PS2116.D33N48   1993
813'.4 – dc20   92–47280

A catalog record for this book is available from the British Library.

ISBN 0-521-41673-6 hardback
ISBN 0-521-42681-2 paperback

Contents

v

Contents

Series Editor's Preface

In literary criticism the last twenty-five years have been particularly fruitful. Since the rise of the New Criticism in the 1950s, which focused attention of critics and readers upon the text itself – apart from history, biography, and society – there has emerged a wide variety of critical methods which have brought to literary works a rich diversity of perspectives: social, historical, political, psychological, economic, ideological, and philosophical. While attention to the text itself, as taught by the New Critics, remains at the core of contemporary interpretation, the widely shared assumption that works of art generate many different kinds of interpretations has opened up possibilities for new readings and new meanings.

Before this critical revolution, many works of American literature had come to be taken for granted by earlier generations of readers as having an established set of recognized interpretations. There was a sense among many students that the canon was established and that the larger thematic and interpretative issues had been decided. The task of the new reader was to examine the ways in which elements such as structure, style, and imagery contributed to each novel's acknowledged purpose. But recent criticism has brought these old assumptions into question and has thereby generated a wide variety of original, and often quite surprising, interpretations of the classics, as well as of rediscovered works such as Kate Chopin's *The Awakening,* which has only recently entered the canon of works that scholars and critics study and that teachers assign their students.

The aim of The American Novel Series is to provide students of American literature and culture with introductory critical guides to American novels and other important texts now widely read and studied. Usually devoted to a single work, each volume begins with an introduction by the volume editor, a distinguished authority on the text. The introduction presents details of the work's composition, publication history, and contemporary reception, as well as a survey of the major critical trends and readings from first publication to the present. This overview is followed by four or five original essays, specifically commissioned from senior scholars of established reputation and from outstanding younger critics. Each essay presents a distinct point of view, and together they constitute a forum of interpretative methods and of the best contemporary ideas on each text.

It is our hope that these volumes will convey the vitality of current critical work in American literature, generate new insights and excitement for students of American literature, and inspire new respect for and new perspectives upon these major literary texts.

Emory Elliott
University of California, Riverside

A Note on the Text

THE EARLIER and later versions of *Daisy Miller: A Study* are not so different as to constitute two different tales, but most scholars see the revised 1909 version as lacking the freshness of the 1878–79 original. Consequently, the contributors to this volume have depended on the story as presented in the Norton Critical Edition of the *Tales of Henry James,* which reproduces the first book edition published by Macmillan in England in 1879. Only a few minor changes differentiate this first book edition from the June and July 1878 *Cornhill* magazine serial. Perhaps because it was written closer to the time when James was working on the so-called New York Edition of *The Novels and Tales* (1907–9), *The Turn of the Screw* was less heavily altered for what James believed to be the definitive edition of his work. The New York version has therefore emerged as *Screw's* standard text, although there are of course some interesting changes that scholars have avidly pursued, especially changes in wording which may affect our interpretation of the characters' history and motivation. The contributors to this volume have depended on the later, 1908 New York Edition as presented in the Norton Critical Edition of *The Turn of the Screw.* Both the Norton editions discuss textual matters and provide the basis for further study of James's revisions, as do some of the materials included in the Bibliography at the end of this volume. These editions were also chosen for their wide availability.

1

Introduction

VIVIAN R. POLLAK

"WE ARE each the product of circumstances and there are tall stone walls which fatally divide us," Henry James wrote to William Dean Howells in March 1877, as they were arguing about the unhappy ending of *The American*. "I suspect it is the tragedies in life that arrest my attention more than the other things and say more to my imagination."[1] From the beginning of his career, James was both fortunate and unfortunate in his critics. Some were hostile, some merely indifferent, still others were bewildered but willing to be instructed by him. His brother William blew hot and cold, while Emily Dickinson succinctly declared her ambivalence. "Of Howells and James," she explained to Thomas Wentworth Higginson, who had just attacked James in print, "one hesitates."[2] Yet in writing to a woman friend several months earlier, the Amherst recluse had commented that "A thousand questions rise to my lips, and as suddenly ebb – for how little I know of you recently – An awkward loneliness smites me – I fear I must ask with Mr. Wentworth [one of the main characters in *The Europeans*], 'Where are our moral foundations?' "[3]

With his hard-to-grasp moral foundations, the early James was criticized for pessimism, for the overrefinement and diffuseness of his style, for what William James called "something cold, thin-blooded and priggish suddenly popping in and freezing the genial current."[4] But he was also praised for his cleverness, "instinct of truth," and "richness of expression" – for his originality, "acute power," for the depth of his characterization, "dramatic ability," gift for rendering talk, cosmopolitanism, Americanness, and for suppressing his own personality.[5] "Henry James waked up all the women with his *Daisy Miller*, the intention of which they miscon-

1

ceived," Howells wrote gleefully to their mutual friend James Russell Lowell in June 1879, a year after the story had first appeared in the *Cornhill* magazine. "And there has been a vast discussion in which nobody felt very deeply, and everybody talked very loudly. The thing went so far that society almost divided itself into Daisy Millerites and anti-Daisy Millerites."[6] Ruefully, James later observed that *Daisy* was "promptly pirated in Boston – a sweet tribute I hadn't yet received and was never again to know." To hear him tell it, James never shook off the story's initial rejection by a Philadelphia publisher who perhaps thought it " 'an outrage on American girlhood.' "[7]

As the chronicler of lives that in the fullest sense fail to occur, maimed lives beset by obscure hurts, James was setting himself against a programmatically optimistic culture. Noted one bemused British critic,

> In his pictures, most passions fade away; most influences fail of their characteristic effect; most comedies are spoiled; most tragedies break down before the tragic crisis; most catastrophes... never come off, while that which fulfils its function most completely in the world is the power, inherent in most of us, to spoil or hamper the life of other people, an agency the conspicuous success of which almost all Mr. James's writings commemorate.[8]

"Mr. James has a sufficient contempt for prettiness and obviousness," explained a more sympathetic Briton, in a review that commented on the touching pathos of *Daisy Miller*. He called it "out and away the best thing of its kind in recent English."[9] Yet when Richard Grant White, an American, discussed the *nouvelle* along with *The Europeans* in the *North American Review* in January 1879, he sensed something vaguely unassimilable and foreign in it. "We do not know a living writer, except Matthew Arnold," White announced, "who produces upon his readers a greater impression of self-knowledge, of self-restraint, or of perpetual self-consciousness." But the review continued,

> Mr. James does not belong to the English school (English and American being in literature but one), but rather to the French. His cast of thought is French; he has the French nicety of taste, the French reserve of manner, dexterity of hand, and fineness of finish; what

wit he has is French, and he is French in the paleness and paucity of his humor.[10]

In sum, James had reason to be leery of his critics, though in Britain, he believed, he had a greater chance of finding the unqualified success that had eluded him in his "less developed" native land.

"I scratch along on this crowded highway of London life & shall probably do so for an indefinite period," an elated James wrote to his boyhood friend Thomas Sergeant Perry in May 1879, in the heady days after *Daisy Miller* had attracted the favorable attention he devoutly courted. "I have got a good deal of fame & hope some day to get a little money. I have had, I think, more success with the dull British public in a few months than with that of my native land in all these long years that I have been scribbling to it."[11] But James, who distrusted mere popularity, also harbored a reserve of authorial bitterness that could erupt at any time. The next year he wrote to Perry, himself a man of letters,

> The hubbub produced by my poor little *Hawthorne* is most ridiculous; my father has sent me a great many notices, each one more abusive & more abject than the others. The vulgarity, ignorance, rabid vanity & general idiocy of them all is truly incredible. But I hold it a great piece of good fortune to have stirred up such a clatter. The whole episode projects a lurid light upon the state of American 'culture', & furnishes me with a hundred wonderful examples, where, before, I had only more or less vague impressions. Whatever might have been my own evidence for calling American taste 'provincial', my successors at least will have no excuse for not doing it.[12]

Challenging the conventional gender expectations of his audience, throughout his career James risked the most public forms of failure. If nothing else, he consistently committed himself to the production of works that were as yet unwritten and on whose successful production he depended for his livelihood. Though he came from a wealthy family and had influential literary connections, until the death of his sister Alice he lived exclusively on the money that he earned and functioned effectively in a demanding literary marketplace on two continents.[13] Thus the James who was exclusively the voice of the very idle rich, who recoiled fastidiously from the deadline-ridden life most of us know, never existed. Of course James's *fantasy* of himself as a man of liberal leisure was very strong. Without denying the shaping power of this fantasy side of James – James freed from social, sexual, and economic imperatives – the best recent criticism has persistently deconstructed the still popular image of James in his ivory tower, splendidly oblivious to any world beyond the self-enclosed one of his rarefied language. But if any single factor links the essays in this collection, it is their continuous awareness of the richness of James's social, sexual, and economic imagination both in and out of his time. For in addressing the anxieties of his contemporaries, he illuminates cultural traditions by which we continue to be haunted.

As James devoted himself to subverting the traditional courtship plot of the Anglo-American novel which necessitated that Christopher Newman positively *must* marry Claire de Cintré, Winterbourne *must* marry Daisy, and the Governess *must* marry the Master, he was accused by reviewers such as Higginson of being betwixt and between. "Mr. James's cosmopolitanism is after all limited," Higginson declared. "To be really cosmopolitan a man must be at home even in his own country."[14] Higginson was not the only critic to find the national and erotic irresolution of James's heroes distasteful. Praised for his delicacy, James was also blamed for lacking robustness. Some readers liked his sexual idealism; others saw him, especially after the work of the 1890s, as a sexual degenerate. Accused of being too much of a gentleman, too much of a scholar, "developing," in the words of Oscar Wilde, but "never arriv[ing] at passion," by which Wilde presumably meant homosexual passion, he was nevertheless the author, in the view of his contemporaries, of novels "like *The Awkward Age,* and *What Marie* [sic] *Knew,* that are as full of the covert suggestion of foulness as the worst French novel of the last forty years. And there is one short story of his, 'The Turn of the Screw', which is a sheer moral horror, like the evil dream of a man under the spell of a deadly drug."[15] Critics troubled by James's deracination and fin-de-siècle pessimism were also responding, in part, to his astute analysis of a sex-gender system in transition. More recent gender critics have debated the extent to which James's thought was implicated in the sexism of his culture. James both feared and delighted in the New Woman who represented radical social change. "Frederick Winterbourne, c'est moi," he might have said. And in so saying, he would have been gainsaying the fact. Though not entirely. Retrospectively, Winterbourne feels compelled to enact the part of a man in love. So too an older James felt compelled to enact the postmortem role of a man in love with his dead cousin Minny Temple, whom he memorialized as the heroine of his youthful scene. "Mary Temple," he crooningly intoned, "radiant and rare, extinguished in her first youth, but after having made an impression on many persons, and on ourselves not least, which was to become in the harmonious circle, for all time, matter of sacred legend and reference, of associated piety."[16]

> "Natural" to an effect of perfect felicity that we were never to see surpassed . . . natural at more points and about more things, with a greater range of freedom and ease and reach of horizon than any of the others dreamed of . . . she was to remain for us the very figure and image of a felt interest in life . . . the supreme case of a taste for life as life, as personal living; of an endlessly active and yet somehow a careless, an illusionless, a sublimely forewarned curiosity about it: something that made her, slim and fair and quick, all straightness and charming tossed head, with long light and yet almost sliding steps and a large light postponing, renouncing laugh, the very muse or amateur priestess of rash speculation. . . . She burned herself out; she died at twenty-four.[17]

Like Winterbourne, James idealized the life that might have been. And in confronting his characters with a resistant environment, social and biological, he lamented their loss of innocence: innocence of erotic negotiation, innocence of physical and moral fear, innocence of economic, sexual, and political compulsion. A realist acquainted with the infinitely painful nuances of romantic nostalgia, James both wished to hearken back to an earlier, simpler time and vehemently rejected myths of lost Edens. The golden age never was, but the golden age might have been. Hence the Jamesian theme of *too little, too late,* which organizes so much of his shorter fiction and which this fiction, with its necessary exclusions, is superbly designed to accommodate. Whatever the sexual ambiguities of the Master himself, and they are many, whatever the manifold deferments of desire in which he himself engaged, the finest Jamesian heroines emerge, in what Robert Weisbuch calls "a world of rooms and rules," as exemplars of the unexpected. They exude the whiff of fresh air, these freedom-loving sisters of Daisy, and are born to defy the erotically conservative antiheroes of an unheroic present. Further, as Kenneth Graham suggests, Daisy's "fluidity, [and] provisionality" correspond to "an underlying view of reality" from which James critiques a thoroughly static, essentialist concept of the self. In his reading, even Winterbourne emerges as something of an enigma.[18]

Like Isabel Archer, the contradictory heroine of James's most complex early novel (1881), Daisy Miller rebukes and justifies the caution of her elders. But whereas Isabel thrives on introspection and is tested by adversity, the younger heroine has only the most rudimentary conception of the social situation that shapes her inner life. Aptly described as an "inscrutable combination of audacity and innocence,"[19] she dies before she can internalize the voices of caution that seek both to confine and to save her. In dying, Daisy escapes Isabel's harsher fate: disappointment, disillusionment, despair. But if it appears that Daisy needs to be saved from herself, Isabel from others, the dichotomy is finally too simple. In suffering and in sacrifice, Isabel lives; in failing to sacrifice or to suffer, Daisy dies. *Portrait* demonstrates the developed depth of James's ambivalence toward those traditionally valid gender roles that Daisy so flagrantly defies. Saved by her early death from the self-revising compromises of moral maturity, she is subjected to relentless scrutiny by such inauthentic arbiters of taste as Mrs. Walker, Mrs. Costello, and (most notably) Frederick Winterbourne, himself a socially liminal figure with an uncertain past.

Yet Daisy is also mindlessly ignored. In the usual course of events, she is ignored by her father, living as he does in a "separate sphere" from the world of women and preoccupied as he is with his lucrative business in Schenectady. Ezra B. Miller has no culture himself, but craves culture for his daughter, who is prone to conspicuous displays of her own beautiful person. Ezra B. Miller exists in the margins of the text. We never see him or hear his voice. At the text's center and virtually throughout the story, Daisy is *startlingly* neglected by her foolish and hypochondriacal mother, a negative role model who wears her daughter's discarded clothing. In the truncated Miller family as we see it in Europe – mother, daughter, and pathetically overindulged younger brother – there is no one who wears the pants. Daisy, however, conjures up the disturbing specter of an erotically aggressive New Woman, whereas Randolph conjures up the no less disturbing specter of a bullying street orphan. He stands in for the disorder of the economically aggressive lower classes.

Timid Mrs. Miller, who rallies slightly to nurse Daisy ineffectually during her daughter's brief but terminal illness, is denied even the dignity of a first name. There is *Ezra B.* Miller. There is *Randolph C.* Miller. There is *Annie P.* Miller, *Daisy* as she was originally and inaptly named. Mrs. Miller is only Mrs. Miller. Not only does Daisy's boldness emerge more vividly against the background of her mother's ineptitude, but Mrs. Miller's passivity seems to necessitate Daisy's daring. As she violates codes of gender-appropriate behavior, some of which prove sensible and others fatal to her rudimentary development, the newly rich new American girl arouses the anxieties of an improvised, impermanent culture in which men like Winterbourne have no obvious compelling economic or social function. Moreover, the family values in James's European social laboratory are quite simple. In *Daisy Miller*, there are no intact families, though the ghost of such intactness haunts the text. As the master of a superficially elegant world whose beautiful surfaces belie bankrupt moral codes, James thrives on the suspension of ordinary family life. Slyly, he teaches us that traditionally gendered syntax no longer signifies sense.

Rejecting the opportunity to heed *any* mentor, Daisy is taken up, snubbed, and summarily dropped by the inflexible American community in Rome, which is edgily hyperconscious of its basic social marginality. Against this mock community she is to some extent defended by her would-be lover, Frederick Winterbourne, a rootless American expatriate who is the story's point-of-view character. Despite his voyeuristic mode, the arid Winterbourne realizes too late that Daisy might have provided him with a reason for being. Alas, Daisy's potential for transforming and redeeming

Winterbourne's aridity is never realized. Her lack of caution and of self-consciousness expose her to an all-too-predictable fate. Daisy Miller, the archetypal bold American girl, the paradoxically frank flirt who possesses "that charm, very hard to express, which we find in an artist's work the first time he has touched his highest mark," ends up transcending national boundaries in her last and finally fixed role as female victim.[20]

Touching *one* of his highest marks in *Daisy Miller*, a story in which lightness of touch and complexity of social insight coexist, James was, it may seem to us, virtually at the beginning of his astonishingly productive career as writer and critic. And yet, in 1878, the thirty-five-year-old James was certainly no newcomer to fiction. Even before the Civil War, according to his friend Thomas Sergeant Perry, young "Harry" James, as he was then called, "was continually writing stories, mainly of a romantic kind. The heroes were for the most part villains, but they were white lambs by the side of the sophisticated heroines, who seemed to have read all Balzac in the cradle and to be positively dripping with lurid crimes." Perry, who was a frequent visitor to the James family home in Newport, recalled that

> H. J. seldom entrusted these early efforts to the criticism of his family – they did not see all he wrote. They were too keen critics, too sharp-witted, to be allowed to handle every essay of this budding talent. Their judgments would have been too true, their comments would have been too merciless; and hence, for sheer self-preservation, he hid a good part of his work from them. Not that they were cruel, far from it. Their frequent solitude in foreign parts, where they had no familiar companions, had welded them together in a way that would have been impossible in America, where each would have had separate distractions of his own. Their loneliness forced them to grow together most harmoniously, but their long exercise in literary criticism would have made them possibly merciless judges of H. J.'s crude beginnings.

Perry, himself an affectionate critic of his friend's shyness, went on to observe that

> H. J.'s spirits were never so high as those of the others. If they had been, he still would have had but little chance in a conflict of wits with them, on account of his slow speech, his halting choice of words and phrases; but as a companion in our walks he was de-

8

lightful. He had plenty of humour, as his books show, and above all he had a most affectionate heart. No one ever had more certain and more unobtrusive kindness than he. He had a certain air of aloofness, but he was not indifferent to those who had no claim upon him, and to his friends he was most tenderly devoted. Those who knew him will not need to be assured of that.[21]

The autobiographical struggle between shyness and boldness that informs *Daisy* figures prominently in other preparatory early works. Throughout most of *Watch and Ward,* for example, the first novel that James subsequently disowned in favor of *Roderick Hudson,* there is no "Daisy" character, but there is a potential Winterbourne. As the story opens – it was serialized in the *Atlantic Monthly* in 1871 and then issued in book form in 1878 – a shy, twenty-nine-year-old bachelor who adopts an elaborately formal manner to conceal his personal insecurity has just been rebuffed by the woman he loves. Determined to give up love forever and to adopt a life of settled cynicism, he instead manages to adopt a desperate twelve-year-old girl whose father, under bizarre circumstances, has just committed suicide. This young girl, Nora Lambert, develops under his tutelage into a charming woman whom he hopes to marry; he rears her with an eye toward this marriage. There are many other plot combinations and character types which need not concern us here, but in the end the pressure of an emerging "Daisy" makes itself felt. Shortly before the novel's conclusion, Nora Lambert flees from her guardian to New York City and to the false embrace of her greedy cousin George Fenton. As Nora begins to suspect him of duplicity, he reminds her that she may have sacrificed her reputation by coming to live with him, however briefly. " 'I confess I don't understand you!' " he exclaims. " 'But the more you puzzle me the more you fascinate me; and the less you like me the more I love you. What has there been, anyway, between you and Lawrence [her guardian]? Hang me if I can understand! Are you an angel of purity, or are you the most audacious of flirts?' " Elements of this foundational story, which strains to reaffirm the value of a "sound, sensible marriage," reappear throughout James's work. "I have begun at the beginning," Roger Lawrence writes to the woman who spurned him. "It will be my own fault if I have not a perfect wife."[22]

Anticipating subsequent Jamesian motifs, *Watch and Ward* is nevertheless unusual in its rush to a "happy" ending (to say nothing of James's bold foregrounding of the incest motif). For throughout his early tales, of which *Daisy Miller* is the exemplary culmination, the sad and the sinister eerily intersect. The Jamesian family romance is an antiromance as well. Thus Daisy's pathetically bare April grave in the fabled Protestant cemetery at Rome is the kind of heartless empty space whose silence reverberates throughout James's early tales of failed courtships and narrowly averted marriages. Often told from a young woman's point of view, these stories move briskly toward startling denouements, typically endings that uncouple. Perhaps few of these heroines, the product of James's American years – he published his first story anonymously in 1864[23] – exhibit that combination of sexual audacity and sexual innocence that caused James to describe Daisy as *inscrutable*. And certainly her unpredictability is essential to her charm. Does she or doesn't she, will she or won't she, Winterbourne wonders obsessively. Her sexuality, he believes, is constantly at issue. Nice girls don't, at least not before they are married. And maybe not even then. Unwilling as he is to risk rejection by Daisy and preoccupied as he is with the culturally inflated issue of her sexual virtue (double standards abound), Winterbourne cedes the erotic field to a lighthearted Italian opportunist. Eventually, he returns to the older married woman in Geneva who occupies only some of his attention and does not genuinely touch his heart. Winterbourne is the bachelor type we recognize elsewhere in James: the man with the empty house on the jolly corner whom life passes by.

With its legacy of easy acclaim, this graceful and thought-provoking 1878 story lived to haunt Henry James who, like his later character Ralph Limbert, always hoped for a "next time."[24] On that supremely happy occasion, his own valuation of his work and the public's would converge. Fabulous riches would descend on the head of the delighted author; on that day, his work would justify his life. Considered as a publishing event, *Daisy Miller* was as close as James ever came to an actual *next time*. First rejected by a Philadelphia publisher and then accepted in Britain by Virginia Woolf's father, Leslie Stephen, the story provided James with access to some of the best houses in London. He dined out, as he proudly wrote his American friend Grace Norton, one hundred and seven times that winter.[25] Perhaps he never felt the degree of disgust for *Daisy* that Walt Whitman entertained for his uncharacteristic and uncharacteristically popular poem "O Captain! My Captain!," but Henry James was never in later years to consider *Daisy Miller* his most sophisticated work. Subject as he was to bouts of self-deprecation and embarrassment, he seems always, like Limbert, to have been in love with the work in progress and the work about to be. *"My work,"* he explained, *"is my salvation."*[26] And yet he believed that fiction writers needed to immerse themselves in experience, that they depended on actual germinal situations for their inspiration.[27] So to live to write was to live a strangely social life: to visit the great houses and to penetrate the relations of persons, whatever their social class, who were radically unlike himself.

By the time James came to publish *The Turn of the Screw* in 1898 – he had begun dictating his works out loud in his polyglot Anglo-American accent in 1897 – he had moved toward an even more intimate identification with his beleaguered and beguiling heroines and toward the further proliferation of subjective moral possibilities. In *The Turn of the Screw,* the conventional norms of interpretation that were already under pressure in *Daisy Miller* have been further exploded. If we have questions about Daisy's response to moral pressure (to say nothing of Winterbourne's sexual indeterminacy), we have more questions about the much-discussed but nameless Governess's construction of reality (to say nothing of the children's). It might almost appear that "every key to interpretation has been lost" and that the story is inscribed on "the fine parchment" of a "missing record."[28] What remains constant in both works, however, is James's intelligent empathy with the situation of women who seek to outwit their cultural fates.

More powerful than Daisy, a survivor with a haunting voice of her own, the Governess of James's most famous ghost story longs for a freer, more self-indulgent, and reckless life. In her hunger to escape her social conditioning and to transgress class barriers, she longs to be an "American." Equally, however, she aspires to uphold the established social order that mandates her sexual and economic martyrdom. Endowed with such sober Victorian virtues as courage, caution, and fidelity to duty, in her zeal to defend herself and her surrogate children against democratic insurrections, she is responsible for the death of one of her beautiful young charges, Miles, and nearly destroys Flora, the other. Like Morgan Moreen's admiring tutor Pemberton in the 1891 story "The Pupil," she reveals how deeply love and death are intertwined in the later Jamesian psyche and how difficult it is to distinguish a ruthless drive toward chaos from a merciful will to order.

But what *is* the Governess's cultural fate? Marriage or madness or silence? Seduction by the Master or evasion of that seduction? Does she perpetuate a past in which children are exploited and their individual needs ignored or inaugurate a more democratic, more genuinely childloving present? And what are we to infer from the fact that she is gainfully and apparently happily employed some nine or ten years after leaving Bly? Apparently she has not been subjected to any social disgrace. Or if she has been, Douglas does not know about it. Certainly she has been able to find another perfectly "respectable" position and has aroused the admiration of Douglas, whom the "I" narrator admires and whom we as readers are encouraged to trust. If the Governess has been unable to resist her cultural fate as Madwoman or Monster Mother and if she has had a public breakdown following her experience at Bly, she has also publicly recovered. But probably such a post-Bly breakdown never occurred; if she suffered a breakdown, it occurred *during* the story and inspired her demonic visions. Killing or eliminating Miles was, from this perspective, effective in her cure. Proceeding further down this road, which eventuates in a sordidly detailed history of child abuse, merely indicates how wide open the interpretative possibilities are. Anything does not go, but almost anything does. For a story with such an elaborate preamble, the conclusion is remarkably absent.

There is also a preamble to the preamble. James's prefaces, of which David McWhirter makes excellent use in his argument *for* the Governess, can also become, like the story itself, a snare "to catch those not easily caught" (120). "The fun," James went on to add maliciously, "of the capture of the merely witless being ever but small." Like James's other statements of authorial intention, the prefaces deepen though they do not solve the mystery of the Governess's history and motivation. In my view, the Governess is herself the patriarchal victim of mother deprivation. She is another one of James's mother-deprived heroines: like Daisy, like Isabel, like Isabel's stepdaughter Pansy Osmond – a line of mother-wounded girls and women (consider poor Maisie Farange) that eventuates in the finally triumphant (but oh how ambiguously) Maggie Verver.[29] But there are elements of the story that would seem to resist my interpretation of the Governess as both victim and victimizer, such as the roadblocking, depsychologizing description of Peter Quint in Chapter 5. There are ways around this materialist description but they can also be experienced as evasions of textual reality. James was determined to thwart ready access to the secrets at Bly, and he succeeded.

At the same time that James seems to inspire a melodramatically polarized mode of interpretation – either the Governess is remarkably virtuous or she is damnably evil – he destabilizes the authoritative class and gender conventions on which the validity of a single, coherent reading depends. Satirizing the melodramatic mentality as it emerges in the Governess's conception of heroic fidelity to duty, whatever the odds, James also ironizes the rush to judgment in particular cases. The characters in the opening frame, for example, are eager for conclusions before they have heard the story proper. But Douglas's promise, " 'You'll easily judge why when you hear. . . . You'll easily judge,' he repeated: *'you* will,' " turns out to be illusory. Neither the "I" narrator nor Douglas himself, the possessor of the story's manuscript, can easily judge. Nor for all her apparent self-righteousness, can the Governess, the author of the manuscript on which the larger story depends. Thus to focus on the Governess as a victim of patriarchal oppression who herself victimizes the youthful and in that sense innocent inheritors of patriarchal privilege may be to ignore the story's texture, whereas to ignore the politics of the Governess's position – a politics brilliantly sketched out for us by Millicent Bell

— is to move beyond the possibility of moral action. McWhirter cautions us against ignoring the voice of the Governess; Bell cautions us against accepting it uncritically.

By the time James came to publish *The Turn of the Screw* in 1898, it might almost have seemed to him and to others that he had permanently abandoned the international theme that had originally made him famous. From this perspective, *The Bostonians,* which had quirkily emerged from his return visit to the land of his birth after a six-year absence, might have reflected both his desire to write "a very American tale" and his farewell to American identity.[30] As a cosmopolitan protomodernist, James was moving away, so the story goes, from an earlier realist or naturalist sense of self as implicated in history. His characters, Edith Wharton protested, were eventually almost severed "from that thick nourishing human air in which we all live and move."[31] Wharton was right to be concerned about James's loss of a nourishing, "explanatory" sense of place. As his brother William often reminded him and as James himself acknowledged in his letters home, there were costs to his physical and psychic liberation from the American scene.[32] But though the flame flickered, especially during the 1890s when he was casting about for new directions and new audiences — witness his persistence in writing for the theater despite the unsuitability of his novels for the stage — James never entirely lost his interest in nationality as a crucial determinant of character. Thus, as Virginia Fowler observes,

> When Henry James visited America in 1904 after a twenty-year absence from the land of his birth, his imagination responded not simply to the plight of America but also to that of the American woman, a figure whom he had used repeatedly in much of his early fiction and recently celebrated anew in *The Wings of the Dove* and *The Golden Bowl.* The "American girl" had been, in fact, the focal point of most of his international fiction, and even when he came to write "a very *American* tale," *The Bostonians,* he noted his conviction that "the situation of women" represented "the most salient and peculiar point in our social life."[33]

Credited by his enabling friend and mentor William Dean Howells with having invented the American girl as a literary type, James found her a uniquely satisfying vehicle for exploring what he viewed as the crude youthful presumptions of American life. "Heiress of all the ages," she was also "the sport of fate."[34] As he explained in *The American Scene,* the 1907 record of his belated reencounter with the land from which, for complex personal and professional reasons, he had, after several false starts, permanently ventured forth,

> What it came to, evidently, was that [the American girl] had been grown in an air in which a hundred of the "European" complications and dangers didn't exist, and in which also she had had to take upon herself a certain training for freedom. It was not that she had had, in the vulgar sense, to "look out" for herself, inasmuch as it was of the very essence of her position not to be threatened or waylaid; but that she could develop her audacity on the basis of her security, just as she could develop her "powers" in a medium from which criticism was consistently absent. Thus she arrived, full-blown, on the general scene, the least criticized object, in proportion to her importance, that had ever adorned it. It would take long to say why her situation, under this retrospect, may affect the inner fibre of the critic himself as one of the most touching on record; he may merely note his perception that she was to have been after all but the sport of fate.[35]

There are a number of remarkable features to this moving passage, including James's presumption in asserting that the American woman was still, in the early twentieth century, an uncriticized type. To be sure, many European observers before James had marveled and recoiled at the greater comparative freedom of America's second sex. Equally, other critics believed that there existed a divorce between business and culture which empowered women as arbiters of genteel taste. Like Daisy's absent father Ezra B. Miller, the American husband was viewed as participating in a social "default"; it was thought that the feminization of American culture deprived both sexes of their opportunities for a healthier, more androgynous ideology and style.[36] But for a comparable passage of shrewd social observation and glaringly self-interested distortion of the facts, one might need to turn to Walt Whitman's 1856 "Open Letter" to Emerson, whom he obsequiously addressed and skewered as his "Master."[37] For surely James must have understood that nineteenth-century American literature had already criticized American women with a vengeance. As a reader and reviser of

15

The Scarlet Letter, to name but a single example, James knew that he was not working in virgin territory. And he knew that he was not the first serious critic to address the so-called woman question, a subject on which his own father had written and lectured extensively.[38] So what could he have meant? By criticism, does he mean such criticism as is offered by intelligent men? Have American women been too partial to their own sex? Have American men been too indulgent? Perhaps he means that his own vision of the complicated relationship between freedom and entrapment has been insufficiently appreciated. The whole passage turns on what is meant by freedom and security, and that is far from clear. Perhaps to be clear is to be *vulgar*, to restrict opportunity, to deny the multivalent possibilities of the visionary gleam, to reduce life's many plots to a single tired tale.

Be that as it may, James's continuing quarrel with "America" helped to sustain his imaginative vitality. And one of the Americas that most interested him was the America of the newly empowered woman – a danger to herself, like Daisy, and a danger to others, like the Governess. One might almost say that the more she was a danger to herself, like Daisy, the less she was a danger to others. This may point to a sadomasochistic cultural dynamic of a peculiarly unpleasant sort. But as James observed in his preface to *The Portrait of a Lady*, "To see deep difficulty braved is at any time, for the really addicted artist, to feel almost even as a pang the beautiful incentive, and to feel it verily in such sort as to wish the danger intensified."[39] Having missed out on the American Civil War – he was drafted in July 1863 but "exempted from military duty by reason of physical disability"[40] – James courted other forms of danger. As did his brother William. "When we entered the mighty colosseum walls," William wrote to his father,

and stood in its mysterious midst with that cold sinister half moon and hardly a star in the deep blue sky – it was all so strange and I must say inhuman and horrible that it felt like a nightmare. Again would I have liked to hear the great curses which you would have spoken. Anti-Christian as I generally am I actually derived a deep comfort from the big black cross that had been planted on that blood-stained soil.[41]

16

Following this visit to the Colosseum with Henry during the fall of 1873, William contracted a mild case of the "Roman fever" to which Daisy Miller succumbed. Unlike Daisy, he saved himself by fleeing a Rome he identified as his brother's territory. Ironically, according to R. W. B. Lewis, "Henry himself, standing at his ease by William's side, had no inkling of his brother's near-collapse and spoke affably to Father of Willy's special pleasure in a 'moonlight walk to . . . the Colisseum.' "[42]

"One's destiny puts on many garments as it goes on shaping itself in secret – let me not cling to any particular fashion," Henry James Senior wrote to his friend and mentor Ralph Waldo Emerson in October 1843.[43] Only six months after the birth of his son and namesake, the Jameses were about to close up their house at 21 Washington Place and sail for Europe. The elder Henry, a philosophical enthusiast and social reformer, had already revisited the home of his Irish ancestors in County Cavan but this was to be his first sojourn abroad as a married man. And it was the first such trip for his wife Mary, who had married rather late in life and already had two sons very close in age. Two more sons were to follow before the birth of the only James daughter, Alice, who was the American girl Henry James knew most intimately before writing *Daisy Miller* and who was arguably the mature woman he knew most intimately (other than his mother) before writing *The Turn of the Screw*.[44]

Recalling her childhood, Alice recalled painful family outings in France, with the heels of Wilky and Bob (the less talented James brothers) digging into her exquisitely sensitive shins.[45] A failed revolutionary who took up the cause of Irish independence toward the end of her shortish life – she was only forty-three when she died of breast cancer in London – Alice James was unfortunately prone to hysterical outbursts, near-suicidal depressions, and mysterious physical maladies, most of them apparently psychosomatic in origin. Like all the James children, she was educated by tutors and governesses, by schools, and by parents who "welcomed almost any influence that might help at all to form their children to civility."[46] There were theaters, and concerts, and museums, in Europe and in the United States. Culture abounded. Potentially,

Alice James was a feminist educator and for several years beginning in late 1875 she participated in a movement to educate women at home through a correspondence course. Her specialty was history. For a Boston-based organization which sought "to induce young ladies to form the habit of devoting some part of every day to study of a systematic and thorough kind," she wrote monthly newsletters to women as far west as California.[47] She was proud of the distance her words traveled, though she is best known today as the author of a diary that remained unpublished until many years after her death.[48] Traumatized by her brother William's marriage to another Alice (Alice Howe Gibbens), her energy sputtered out. During the summer of 1878 she suffered yet another nervous breakdown from which she never fully recovered. In her own words, "the dark waters" rolled over her.[49] In Henry's words, "In our family group girls seem scarcely to have had a chance."[50] But to say this is to read staunch Alice's sad fate back into her more hopeful beginnings. And the beginnings were, as beginnings often are, hopeful.

" 'The flesh said, It is for me, and the spirit said, It is for me,' " Henry Senior charmingly told Emerson about his first meeting with his future wife.[51] Though also attracted to her younger sister Catherine, he came to believe that it had been an undisputed case of love at first sight. For her part, when Mary Robertson Walsh married her brother's passionate friend in July 1840, she had already broken with longstanding family tradition by abandoning her membership in the Murray Street Presbyterian Church. Her fiancé's bold liberal rhetoric was more persuasive. Both Henry Senior and her brother Hugh had been students at the Princeton Theological Seminary. Together they had decided to leave the Seminary and Calvinist orthodoxy behind for freer modes of thought. Because of Henry Senior's vehement anticlericalism, the Jameses were married in her mother's Washington Square parlor by the mayor of New York. Her father, a successful cotton merchant, had died suddenly when she was ten. This loss intensified both her fear of marriage and her need to control the people she loved. At thirty, Mary was married late to a man slightly younger than herself who was missing most of one leg. Probably his lameness appealed to her. "My occupations are all indoor," he wrote to Emerson in March 1842, inviting him to call, "so that I am generally at home – always in the evenings."[52] Despite Henry Senior's emotional volatility, his handicap, in limiting his physical mobility, stabilized their relationship and created a more egalitarian household. Family lore contrasted his intellectual brilliance with her physical robustness. "The poor old mater wears well I am happy to say," Mary wrote blithely to William at a time when everyone else in the family was ailing. "Strong in the back, strong in the nerves, and strong in the legs so far, and equal to her day."[53] "Mother is recovering from one of her indispositions," a hypochondriacal William noted somewhat enviously, "which she bears like an angel, doing any amount of work at the same time, putting up cornices and raking out the garret-room like a little buffalo."[54] Formidably cheerful, she was, a grateful Henry Senior explained condescendingly, "not to me 'a liberal education,' intellectually speaking, as some one has said of his wife, but she really did arouse my heart, early in our married life, from its selfish torpor, and so enabled me to become a man."[55]

In any event, as Lewis has observed, "Henry James, Sr., was married, but he could hardly be said to have settled down. Over the next year and a half, James changed his and Mary's living place not less than five times."

They spent some months with James's mother in the old Albany home. They took rooms in the expensive and showy Astor House in New York City. They rented a house at 5 Washington Square, not far from the Walshes. They returned to the Astor House, and here on January 11, 1842, their first child was born, and was named William, after his grandfather, great-greatfather, and uncle. At the same moment, Henry bought from his brother John Barber James, for the impressive sum of $18,000, a three-story brick house at 21 Washington Place, a quiet street that runs west from Broadway three blocks to the square. This was the first house of James's own; and here Henry Junior was born on April 15, 1843, just fifteen months younger – as he was given to remarking – than William. But soon the father was wondering aloud whether he might not be wise to find "a little nook in the country," perhaps in Connecticut. By October 1843, he had sold the New York house and was off

19

with his wife and their two children for an indeterminate stay in Europe.[56]

The story of Henry Senior's "vastation" in England in May 1844 – it was a combined religious conversion and panic attack – has been told many times, most notably by the sufferer himself:

> When I sat down to dinner on that memorable chilly afternoon in Windsor, [I felt my ego] serene and unweakened by the faintest breath of doubt; before I rose from table, it had inwardly shrivelled to a cinder. One moment I devoutly thanked God for the inappreciable boon of selfhood; the next, that inappreciable boon seemed to me the one thing damnable on earth, seemed a literal nest of hell within my own entrails.[57]

> To all appearance it was a perfectly insane and abject terror, without ostensible cause, and only to be accounted for, to my perplexed imagination, by some damnéd shape squatting invisible to me within the precincts of the room, and raying out from his fetid personality influences fatal to life. The thing had not lasted ten seconds before I felt myself a wreck; that is, reduced from a state of firm, vigorous, joyful manhood to one of almost helpless infancy. The only self-control I was capable of exerting was to keep my seat. I felt the greatest desire to run incontinently to the foot of the stairs and shout for help to my wife, – to run to the roadside even, and appeal to the public to protect me; but by an immense effort I controlled these frenzied impulses, and determined not to budge from my chair till I had recovered my lost self-possession. This purpose I held to for a good long hour, as I reckoned time, beat upon meanwhile by an ever-growing tempest of doubt, anxiety, and despair, with absolutely no relief from any truth I had ever encountered save a most pale and distant glimmer of the divine existence, when I resolved to abandon the vain struggle, and communicate without more ado what seemed my sudden burden of inmost, implacable unrest to my wife.[58]

Following this horrific, delusional episode, which anticipates the psychological terror of *The Turn of the Screw*, he was pulled from severe depression by a Mrs. Chichester, whom he met at a health resort. She introduced him to the writings of the Swedish mystic Emanuel Swedenborg (1688–1772). This is not the place to expatiate on the elder James's philosophical indebtedness to Swedenborg or on the virulent anticlericalism that caused him to attack the New Church, or Church of the New Jerusalem, as "only on the part of its movers a strike for higher wages." He himself, in a more detailed description of the *vastation* (a Swedenborgian term he first heard from Mrs. Chichester) wrote that "Now, to make a long story short, this ghastly condition of mind continued with me, with gradually lengthening intervals of relief, for two years, and even longer."[59] Thus his recovery of psychic equilibrium and conversion to a more robust sense of self (or selflessness, as he might have said) was far from instantaneous. "The main philosophic obligation we owe to Swedenborg," he later wrote, "is his clearly identifying the evil principle in existence with selfhood." "Self-sufficiency," he believed, was "the only evil known to the spiritual universe."[60]

Post*vastation*, the elder Henry suffered from heightened nervousness when called upon to travel from home without the support and immediate presence of his family, especially his wife. Alice recalled in her diary "Father's sudden returns at the end of 36 hours, having left to be gone a fortnight, with Mother beside him holding his hand and we five children pressing close round him 'as if he had just been saved from drowning,' and he pouring out, as he alone could, the agonies of desolation thro' which he had come."[61] Homesick first for his mother Catherine Barber James and then for his wife, the elder Henry passed along a tendency to agoraphobia (literally, "fear of the marketplace") to his son William.[62] But in the end, Henry James Senior's reading of Swedenborg reinforced his innate sociability. If as husband and father he sometimes felt trapped by the demands of other strong personalities, he nevertheless was thoroughly devoted to his wife and children. In fact both he and Mary James strove to define a family culture in which unhappiness was equated with sinfulness. The chronic illnesses of William, Henry, and Alice – William's eyes, Henry's back, Alice's head, as he once put it – were sore temptations for both Henry Senior and Mary James to commit the selfishness and consequent sin of anxiety. Henry Senior had been overtly rebellious as a youth. William, Henry, and Alice ailed. Thus, the father's attempts to banish "sin," on which the mother also insisted, were not successful.

The James children ailed but they also went to Europe. And on some occasions, they went to Europe as adults *because* they ailed.

Within the James family, ailing justified the expense of the trip. The pattern originated with the elder Henry who, though he was "leisured for life" thanks to a large inheritance, advanced ill health as a justification for his 1843 European sojourn. "I think it probable I shall winter in some mild English climate – Devonshire, perhaps," he explained to Emerson, "and go on with my studies as at home. My chest is in an unsound condition someway, and if I can find a superior climate for it in England than I have at home, I think I shall then be much furthered also in my pursuits."[63] Returning to the United States in the summer of 1845 – Garth Wilkinson was born in July – restless, lame, genial Henry Senior divided his time for the next several years between Albany, in the house of his mother, and New York City, where for part of the time they lived with Mary's family, the Walshes. By the summer of 1847 – Robertson had been born the previous year – the Jameses were living in an apartment on Fifth Avenue. And by the spring of 1848, they had bought a house on West Fourteenth Street, where they were mainly to live for the next seven years. In the summers they enjoyed fresher country air. Meanwhile, according to one estimate, the older boys, William and Henry, "were exposed to ten or more schools and a dozen or more chief teachers in the eight metropolitan years."[64]

"Nature and society should have no power to identify me with a particular potato-patch, and a particular family of mankind all my days,"[65] the elder James declared in print in the mid 1850s, a time when he was also publicly declaring himself against formal education for women, whom he pronounced "inferior to man ... inferior in intellect, and ... inferior in physical strength."[66] Then, not clinging to any particular fashion, James took his family to Europe for a three-year stay, from the summer of 1855 to the summer of 1858. The Jameses hoped to provide their children (especially the boys) not only with the opportunity to study French and German but also with "a better sensuous education" than they were likely to get in New York.[67] Additionally, as William was just entering his teens, James was concerned about losing control over his children to the streets of New York. Taking his brood to Europe and transforming them into "hotel children," he cut them off from presumably raucous peers. Henry Senior had reason to be wary of the streets. He had been somewhat addicted to alcohol by the time he was ten and lost a leg during his teens while experimenting with a turpentine-powered balloon. The balloon was propelled by a turpentine-soaked piece of hemp, which eventually landed in and ignited a stable. Henry attempted to extinguish the fire but alas, in the effort, his trousers were set ablaze. There were two amputations of his gangrened leg, both of them above the knee. As a boy, he was a practiced thief from his father's silver drawer and from his mother's larder. Later he understood the dangers of rebellion against parental authority and of youthful high spirits. In the 1850s, so far as we can tell, his stalwart and beloved wife willingly dislocated her household from one continent to another to help combat such tendencies. These dislocations were eased by the presence of her sister, Aunt Kate Walsh, who helped to manage the children. (Aunt Kate had resumed her original name after a brief, and very late, marriage.) And there was additional household help wherever they went. For the trip to Europe in the summer of 1855, for example, they took with them from New York Mademoiselle Annette Godefroi, a French maid. And soon there was an Italian courier as well.

When shortly after their arrival in England Henry Junior developed a case of malaria, he complicated the family association of Europe with health restoration. He was borne from Lyons to Geneva, as he recalled in his autobiography *A Small Boy and Others*, "stretched at my ease on a couch formed by a plank laid from seat to seat and covered by a small mattress and other draperies; an indulgence founded on my visitation of fever, which, though not now checking our progress, assured me, in our little band, these invidious luxuries." So for James it was "the romance of travel." In his "absurdly cushioned state," he absorbed "by a long slow swig that testified to some power of elbow, a larger draught of the wine of perception than any I had ever before owed to a single throb of that faculty." To his enchanted recollection, what the "small sick boy" propped up on his elbow then saw was "a castle and a ruin." This conversion of sickness into vision made a bridge, he concluded, "over to more things than I then knew."[68]

In later years, Alice James described herself as having been cut off from a normal girlhood by the extraordinary nomadism of her youth. "What enrichment of mind & memory can children have without continuity & if they are torn up by the roots every little while as we were," she wrote William in 1888. "Of all things don't make the mistake wh. brought about our rootless & accidental childhood."[69] But Alice's destabilizing past was the novelist's education into paradox. "The literal," he insisted, "played in our education as small a part as it perhaps ever played in any, and we wholesomely breathed inconsistency and ate and drank contradictions." More ambiguously, he added,

> The presence of paradox was so bright among us – though fluttering ever with as light a wing and as short a flight as need have been – that we fairly grew used to allow, from an early time, for the so many and odd declarations we heard launched, to the extent of happily "discounting" them; the moral of all of which was that we need never fear not to be good enough if we were only social enough: a splendid meaning indeed being attached to the latter term.[70]

If sociability was to be the family watchword, neither Henry nor Alice could measure up to their brother William's exalted standard. Henry was inclined to be withdrawn and somewhat morose, whereas William proudly announced, "*I* play with boys who curse and swear!" "He was always," Henry recorded proudly and plangently, "round the corner and out of sight."[71]

For Henry these "bewildered and brooding years" led to a deeper understanding of human complexity, whereas Alice, a nervous invalid for most of her adult life, became cynical, morbid, and helplessly dependent: first on her parents and then, following their deaths, on her loving companion Katharine Loring. "My London life flows evenly along, making, I think, in various ways more and more of a Londoner of me," Henry was writing to William by the end of January 1878. "If I keep along here patiently for a certain time I rather think I shall become a (sufficiently) great man."[72] Thus, as the pace of William's courtship of the formidably competent Alice Howe Gibbens quickened, during the winter of 1878 Henry was creating, with his character Daisy Miller, a countertype to his sister, an anti-Alice who shines forth as an optimistic, radiantly self-confident and surpassingly independent spirit. In contrast to Alice – brooding, brilliant, spectacularly thwarted Alice – Daisy was "pure poetry," a being who believed in the endless possibilities of the human spirit and who paid for this belief with her young life. While both of her brothers were forging ahead, William with personal and Henry with professional success, Alice, who came to call herself an "unsentimental spinster," was, during "that hideous summer of '78" going down to the deep sea and succumbing to the dark waters of nervous collapse.[73]

Following the death of her father in December 1882 – she had been keeping house for him and nursing him through his last illness as he starved himself to death – Alice James moved to England in late 1884 with her beloved nurse-companion Katharine Loring.[74] After nine bedridden weeks in London near Henry's Bolton Street flat, she settled first at Bournemouth, and then returned to London where, insofar as she could, she flourished under Henry's tenderly watchful eye. In many ways, he was the ideal brother: considerate and undemanding, entertaining and worldly. Through Henry, Alice began to be courted by people who were eager to know the only sister of a literary lion.

By the time that James came to write *The Turn of the Screw*, his parents and brother Garth Wilkinson were long since dead, Alice had been dead for more than five years, and James himself had not been back to the United States for a decade and a half. "I suspect it is the tragedies in life that arrest my attention more than the other things and say more to my imagination," James had explained to Howells in 1877. Certainly this self-assessment is borne out by *The Turn of the Screw*, the best known, though not the first, of his ghost stories. Whatever the sources of the tale, and they are many – ranging from traditional Christmas romp through psychiatric case history – *The Turn of the Screw* remains one of the most profound analyses of "the situation of women" in American literature.[75] Childless himself and, according to some, not attracted to children in life, James's textual analysis of the situation of childhood draws on the acutest of his early memories. In *The Turn of the Screw*, he pits the Governess against the children – the Governess who, in certain respects, is little more than a child herself.

And a deprived one at that. His admiration for Alice, whom he once described as his most important social resource,[76] influenced the tale, as did his understanding of the traumatic perpetuity of childhood experience into adulthood. During her lifetime, Alice James broke into print just once: The comic intrusion of an American mother and daughter into her boardinghouse prodded her to write to *The Nation,* ostensibly on the satiric subject of national differences.[77] But Alice James never had her full say on the subject of the nineteenth-century American female tradition, with its emphasis on the primacy of the mother. Writing the larger story of this tradition was left to Henry. And he proceeded through indirection.[78]

Focusing on the interpretative irresolution of *Daisy Miller,* Kenneth Graham reminds us of the poetry of James's language. In his attentiveness to Daisy as a physical being positioned against the landscape and forming part of it, Graham evokes the kind of inner life we might impute to her were James more committed to an essentialist view of character. His essay causes us to regret the loss of so much elusive loveliness. For Robert Weisbuch, Winterbourne's character is both knowable and reprehensible, Daisy's comparatively slighter. Weisbuch studies Winterbourne studying Daisy. The inner life in his analysis belongs to a man who is the prisoner of gender. Weisbuch suggests that James distances himself from Winterbourne's sexism, and notes some of the ways in which James is implicated in the polarities of a perhaps unresolvable ideological debate. Millicent Bell locates the Governess squarely in Victorian England. She argues from the text to the situation of governesses in the 1840s, the Brontë Decade, and from the situation of governesses to the text. This historical background may support readings which resist the Governess's point of view and undermine her credibility as a narrator. David McWhirter, on the other hand, sees the Governess as a more reliable figure, though he responds amply to the contradiction between femininity and authority that, he shows, informs this multifaceted and endlessly puzzling tale. Taken together, these essays illustrate the continuing vitality of Henry James in our time. One of the most intellectually challenging American writers, he has persistently attracted readers with a highly developed appetite for moral and psychological ambiguity. In varying degrees, these essays are self-consciously skeptical of their own ends; positioned firmly in James country, they recognize the limitations of final pronouncements.

NOTES

1. Henry James, in *Henry James: The Critical Heritage*, ed. Roger Gard (New York: Barnes & Noble, 1968), p. 44.
2. Emily Dickinson, in *The Letters of Emily Dickinson*, ed. Thomas H. Johnson, 3 vols. (Cambridge: Harvard University Press, 1958), vol. 2, p. 649, December 1879. For Higginson's estimate of James at this time, see "Henry James, Jr.," in *The Question of Henry James: A Collection of Critical Essays*, ed. F. W. Dupee (New York: Henry Holt, 1945), pp. 1–5.
3. Dickinson, *Letters*, vol. 2, p. 647. The friend was Elizabeth Holland.
4. William James, in Gard, *The Critical Heritage*, p. 28.
5. See Gard, *The Critical Heritage*, pp. 54, 24, 31, 39, 38, 26, 47, 53, 54.
6. William Dean Howells, in Gard, *The Critical Heritage*, p. 74.
7. The quotations are from the New York Edition preface to *Daisy Miller: A Study*, in *Tales of Henry James*, ed. Christof Wegelin (New York: Norton, 1984), p. 369. Subsequent references to this edition will be provided parenthetically in the text.
8. R. H. Hutton, in Gard, *The Critical Heritage*, p. 88.
9. W. E. Henley, in Gard, *The Critical Heritage*, p. 54.
10. Richard Grant White, in Gard, *The Critical Heritage*, pp. 56–7.
11. James, in Gard, *The Critical Heritage*, p. 79.
12. Ibid., p. 87.
13. On the entrepreneurial James, see Michael Anesko, *''Friction with the Market'': Henry James and the Profession of Authorship* (New York: Oxford University Press, 1986). Following the death of his father in 1882, James bestowed his share of the inheritance on Alice. In 1893 the inheritance reverted to him.
14. Higginson, in Dupee, *The Question of Henry James*, p. 4. On erotic irresolution, see p. 5.
15. Harriet Waters Preston, in the *Atlantic*, January 1903; reprinted in Gard, p. 333. The review begins, ''Time was when to receive a package containing new books both by William Dean Howells and Henry James would have been a delightful and even exciting event. Such

time was in the last century and ominously near a generation ago."
The new James book was *The Wings of the Dove.*

16. James, *A Small Boy and Others,* in *Henry James: Autobiography,* ed. Frederick W. Dupee (Princeton: Princeton University Press, 1983), p. 10.
17. James, *Notes of a Son and Brother,* in *Autobiography,* pp. 283–4.
18. See pp. 36 and 66 below.
19. James, *Daisy Miller: A Study,* in *Tales of Henry James,* ed. Wegelin, p. 32. Subsequent quotations from the story are taken from this edition. Page numbers will be provided parenthetically in the text.
20. James, *Hawthorne,* in *Literary Criticism: Essays on Literature, American Writers, English Writers,* ed. Leon Edel (New York: Library of America, 1984), vol. 1, pp. 401–2.
21. Thomas Sergeant Perry, as quoted in Percy Lubbock, *Letters of Henry James,* 2 vols. (New York: Charles Scribner's Sons, 1920), vol. 1, pp. 8–9.
22. James, *Watch and Ward* (New York: Grove Press, 1959). In his introduction to this edition, Leon Edel speculates on some of the autobiographical significance of the character groupings. The quotations are from pp. 226, 186, and 53.
23. "A Tragedy of Error" appeared in the *Continental Monthly* in February. The heroine Hortense Bernier attempts to have her husband murdered but succeeds only in killing her lover.
24. See "The Next Time," in Henry James, *The Figure in the Carpet and Other Stories* (New York: Viking Penguin, 1986), pp. 307–53. The story was first published in 1895 in the *Yellow Book* and was reprinted in Scribner's New York Edition (1907–9) of the collected works.
25. James, in *Henry James: Letters,* ed. Leon Edel, 4 vols. (Cambridge, Mass.: Harvard University Press, 1975), vol. 2, p. 240.
26. James, as quoted in Leon Edel, *Henry James: The Untried Years, 1843–1870* (New York: J.B. Lippincott, 1953), p. 211.
27. In the prefaces to *Daisy Miller* and *The Turn of the Screw,* for example, James described gathering the "germs" of both stories from stories that were told to him. For the preface to *Daisy Miller,* see *Tales of Henry James,* pp. 368–70. For the preface to *The Turn of the Screw,* see *The Turn of the Screw,* ed. Robert Kimbrough (New York: Norton, 1966), pp. 117–18. See also James's letter to A. C. Benson, pp. 107–8. Quotations from *The Turn of the Screw* are taken from this edition. Page numbers will be cited parenthetically in the text.
28. James, preface to "The Pupil," in *Tales,* p. 379.
29. For an insightful theoretical analysis of the possible ramifications of

mother deprivation in *Portrait,* see Beth Sharon Ash, "Frail Vessels
and Vast Designs: A Psychoanalytic Portrait of Isabel Archer," in *New
Essays on The Portrait of a Lady,* ed. Joel Porte (New York: Cambridge
University Press, 1990), pp. 123–62.

30. James returned to the United States in early November 1881 and his
mother died suddenly of a heart attack at the end of January. Returning to London in May, he was urgently summoned back by Alice
in mid-December. Having no desire to live without his "dear Mary,"
Henry James Senior had slowly starved himself to death. By one day,
the younger Henry arrived too late for his father's funeral.

31. Edith Wharton, as quoted in Millicent Bell, *Meaning in Henry James*
(Cambridge: Harvard University Press, 1991), p. 204.

32. See, for example, James's letter of June 8, 1879, in which he identifies
with those who have lived too long in foreign parts. *Henry James:
Letters,* vol. 2, pp. 239–40. On William as critic, see R. W. B. Lewis,
The Jameses: A Family Narrative (New York: Farrar, Straus & Giroux,
1991), pp. 298–302 and *passim.*

33. Virginia C. Fowler, *Henry James's American Girl: The Embroidery on
the Canvas* (Madison: University of Wisconsin Press, 1984), p. 4. Actually, in August 1904 James was returning to the United States after
a twenty-*one* year absence. Following his father's death, he had returned to England in August 1883.

34. For the ideological context of the James–Howells relationship, see
Paul John Eakin, *The New England Girl: Cultural Ideals in Hawthorne,
Stowe, Howells, and James* (Athens: University of Georgia Press, 1976).
For Howells on James, see *Discovery of a Genius: William Dean Howells
and Henry James,* ed. Albert Mordell (New York: Twayne, 1961).

35. James, *The American Scene* (Bloomington: Indiana University Press,
1968), p. 348.

36. For a fuller discussion of these matters, see Ann Douglas, *The Feminization of American Culture* (New York: Alfred A. Knopf, 1977), and
Ross Posnock, *The Trial of Curiosity: Henry James, William James, and
the Challenge of Modernity* (New York: Oxford University Press, 1991),
pp. 259–62 and *passim.* Posnock views James as "deeply skeptical of
the unconditioned sense of freedom implicit in the feminist goal of
'self-direction' " (p. 260).

37. Walt Whitman, "Open Letter to Emerson," in *Leaves of Grass,* ed.
Sculley Bradley and Harold W. Blodgett (New York: Norton, 1965),
pp. 732–41.

38. For James's relationship to American women writers and for his
father's gender critique, see Alfred Habegger, *Henry James and the*

"Woman Business" (New York: Cambridge University Press, 1989). Habegger suggests that "From the beginning the wild card in James's conservative approach to women was a deep identification with them" and that "The gender-based ideology that is implicit in the novels of the major phase became queerly explicit after James's visit to the United States in 1904–5. His essays on the speech and manners of American women that appeared in *Harper's Bazaar* in 1906 and 1907 brought his lifelong antifeminism to the surface more clearly than any other public writing of his" (pp. 233, 235).

39. James, "Preface to *The Portrait of a Lady*," in *French Writers, Other European Writers, Prefaces to the New York Edition* (New York: Library of America, 1984), p. 1079.

40. See Charles and Tess Hoffman, "Henry James and the Civil War," *New England Quarterly* 62 (December 1989), 529.

41. William James, quoted in Lewis, *The Jameses*, p. 237.

42. Lewis, *The Jameses*, p. 237. For a fuller discussion of competition between the two brothers at this time, see Leon Edel, *Life of Henry James: The Conquest of London, 1870–1881* (New York: J. B. Lippincott, 1962), pp. 135–56.

43. Henry James, Senior, quoted in Robert C. Le Clair, *Young Henry James: 1843–1870* (New York: Bookman, 1955), p. 27.

44. For discussions of the life and cultural significance of Alice James see Jean Strouse, *Alice James: A Biography* (Boston: Houghton Mifflin, 1980); Ruth Bernard Yeazell, "Introduction," *The Death and Letters of Alice James* (Berkeley: University of California Press, 1981); *The Diary of Alice James*, ed. Leon Edel (New York: Dodd, Mead, 1964).

45. For an excellent study of the younger brothers that distinguishes nicely between them, see Jane Maher, *Biography of Broken Fortunes: Wilky and Bob, Brothers of William, Henry, and Alice James* (Hamden, Conn.: Archon, 1986).

46. Henry James, *A Small Boy and Others*, in *Henry James: Autobiography*, ed. Dupee, p. 18.

47. On the Society to Encourage Studies at Home, see Strouse, *Alice James*, pp. 170–6.

48. Alice began to keep a diary in May 1889, when her beloved companion Katharine Loring had departed for a three-year stay in America. Loring, also a Bostonian, was needed by her own family and had returned to the United States in August 1887. Alice's diary, beginning "I think that if I get into the habit of writing a bit about what happens, or rather doesn't happen, I may lose a little of the sense of loneliness and desolation which abides with me," was begun during this ab-

sence. After Alice's death, Katharine arranged for a private printing of four copies in 1894: one for herself, and one each for Henry, William, and Robertson. Henry's distress with and destruction of the diary is described in Strouse, pp. 319–23. The diary was more formally and widely published in 1934 under the auspices of Robertson's daughter, Mary James Vaux. *Alice James: Her Brothers—Her Journal,* edited by Anna Robertson Burr and published in New York by Dodd, Mead, was widely reviewed and well received.

49. Alice James, quoted in F. O. Matthiessen, *The James Family: A Group Biography* (New York: Alfred A. Knopf, 1947), p. 273.

50. Henry James, to Mary James Vaux, his niece, quoted in *The Diary of Alice James,* p. 8.

51. Henry James, Senior, quoted in Matthiessen, *The James Family,* p. 6.

52. Henry Senior, in Matthiessen, *The James Family,* p. 40.

53. Mary Walsh James, quoted in Howard M. Feinstein, *Becoming William James* (Ithaca: Cornell University Press, 1984), p. 192.

54. William James, in Feinstein, *Becoming William James,* p. 193.

55. Henry Senior, following his wife's death, to Henry Junior, quoted in Matthiessen, *The James Family,* p. 129. Others were less kind. According to Lilla Cabot Perry, the "poky banality of the James house" was "ruled by Mrs. James . . . HJ's father used to limp in and out and never seemed really to 'belong' to his wife or Miss Walsh, large florid stupid seeming ladies. . . . James's mother (even to my own perception as a child) was the very incarnation of *banality* and his aunt Miss Walsh . . . was not much better. His father always seemed to me genial and delightful . . . but he seemed to me out of place in that stiff stupid house in Cambridge." Quoted in Strouse, *Alice James,* p. 44.

56. Lewis, *The Jameses,* p. 45.

57. Henry Senior, *Society the Redeemed Form of Man,* quoted in Matthiessen, *The James Family,* p. 166.

58. Henry Senior, *Society the Redeemed,* in Matthiessen, *The James Family,* p. 161.

59. Henry Senior, in Matthiessen, *The James Family,* p. 161.

60. Quoted in *Henry James Senior: A Selection of His Writings,* ed. Giles Gunn (Chicago: American Library Association, 1974), pp. 65, 151.

61. Alice James, *The Diary,* pp. 57–8.

62. For a stimulating discussion of the relationship between market anxieties, domesticity, and agoraphobia, see Gillian Brown, *Domestic Individualism: Imagining Self in Nineteenth-Century America* (Berkeley: University of California Press, 1990), especially chap. 6, "The Empire of Agoraphobia."

31

63. Henry Senior, quoted in Ralph Barton Perry, *The Thought and Character of William James*, 2 vols. (Boston: Little, Brown, 1935), vol. 1, p. 50. The fullest discussion of the politics of invalidism in the James family is Feinstein, *Becoming William James*. Feinstein also provides an extensive discussion of the family finances which includes, as he views it, the family scandal: William of Albany's will.

64. Lewis, *The Jameses*, p. 72.

65. Henry Senior, quoted in Habegger's incisive chap. 2, "The Lessons of the Father: Henry James, Sr., on Sexual Difference," p. 33.

66. Henry Senior, quoted in Strouse, *Alice James*, p. 45. The article on "Woman and the 'Woman's Movement' " appeared in March 1853 in *Putnam's Monthly* magazine. He further explained that woman was above all a " 'form of personal affection . . . Her aim in life is . . . simply to love and bless man.' " More generally, Strouse provides an extremely cogent analysis of Henry Senior's gender arrogance and anxiety in its cultural context and in its negative impact on Alice.

67. Henry Senior, quoted in Matthiessen, *The James Family*, p. 45, letter of August 1849. "My wife and I are obliged," he wrote, "so numerous has waxed our family – to enlarge our house in town, and get a country house for the summer. These things look expensive and temporary to us, besides being an additional care; and so, looking upon our four stout boys, who have no play-room within doors, and import shocking bad manners from the street, with much pity, we gravely ponder whether it would not be better to go abroad for a few years with them, allowing them to absorb French and German and get a better sensuous education than they are likely to get here. To be sure, this is but a glimpse of our ground of proceeding – but perhaps you know some decisive word which shall dispense us from any further consideration of the subject."

68. James, *A Small Boy and Others*, pp. 160–1. Interestingly, he believed that the malaria was American in origin, having been "perversely absorbed (probably on Staten Island upwards of a year before)" (p. 158).

69. Alice James, in *The Death and Letters*, p. 148.

70. Henry James, *Small Boy*, pp. 123–4.

71. James, *Small Boy*, pp. 147, 8.

72. James, *Letters*, vol. 2, p. 150.

73. Alice James, in Matthiessen, *The James Family*, p. 273. Evidently both Alice and Daisy were each and in very different ways resisting conventional gender expectations, but their differences are otherwise more striking than their similarities.

74. Following the death of Mary James, Alice and her father had at first seemed to thrive while depending on each other. They moved into a smaller, more convenient house on Beacon Hill while Alice forged ahead with building a large summer house at Manchester-by-the-Sea, north of Boston. At Manchester, "Henry Sr. got up between five and six every morning and wrote until one" (Strouse, p. 205). It is unclear at what point he began to determine not to live, though his condition was grave by November. Alice, too, collapsed in November, rallied, and collapsed again in December, the month of his death. She entered the Adams Nervine Asylum in May 1883, for " 'nervous people who are not insane' " (Strouse, *Alice James*, p. 221), all of them women.

75. The most thoroughgoing analysis of *"The Turn of the Screw* and Alice James" is by Oscar Cargill; it first appeared in *PMLA* 78 (June 1963) and was reprinted in *Screw*, ed. Kimbrough, pp. 145–65. Cargill attributes the story's ambiguity to James's need to conceal Alice's identity. "James's 'strategy,' " he believes, "consisted in overlaying his real story with another which might, with plausibility, be construed as a ghost story. The limitations of that 'strategy' are, however, that it temporarily confounds the acute and perceptive and, like life, rewards the obtuse and conventional. Thanks to it, *The Turn of the Screw* continues to be misread as a 'pure ghost story' " (146).

76. See James's letter of March 9 to Francis Boott, in *Letters*, vol. 3, pp. 381–2. He speaks of Alice as "the consolation . . . in disappointment and depression, of my own existence. . . . To me her death makes a great and sad personal difference – her talk, her company, her association and admirable acute mind and large spirit were so much the best thing I have, of late years, known here." See also the letter to Henrietta Reubell of March 15, quoted in Strouse, *Alice James*, p. 317, in which he eulogizes Alice as "not only my nearest and dearest relation, but . . . a cherished social relation, as it were, as well, and a great – on the whole my greatest, social resource."

77. For Alice's *Nation* note, which was published anonymously, see Strouse, pp. 289–90.

78. Most readers of *The Turn of the Screw* know that the Governess's father was eccentric and that she was receiving disturbing news from home. But where, we may well ask, is the Governess's mother? Criticism has been silent on this telling point, as is the story itself.

Daisy Miller:
Dynamics of an Enigma

KENNETH GRAHAM

I N *Daisy Miller*, as so often in Henry James, the central presence of indecision provides the decisiveness and energy of the narrative. Winterbourne's bafflement over what to make of Daisy's contradictory behavior, and the reader's double bafflement over what to make of Daisy and of Winterbourne's view of Daisy, indicate the tale's thematic, which I take to be concerned with the unknowable nature of human character, the slipperiness of all forms of human judgment, and the unresolvable dialectic between the impulse to discriminate, which connotes intelligence, and the impulse to sympathize, which connotes love. But what is of equal interest is something more strictly procedural than thematic: that is, how the tale deploys its strategies for narrative interest and reader involvement around this enigmatic and apparently nebulous center, the unknowableness of Daisy. In pursuing this interest, I wish to steer a deliberate course between the conventional moral or psychological thematic approach – which has overwhelmingly dominated criticism of *Daisy Miller* until now – and the (to me) unappealingly airless abstraction of the strictly narratological approach. By closely analyzing the process of the narrative in terms of the reading experience, yet avoiding the private vocabulary of narratology, I hope to relocate its thematic more firmly within the dynamics of the text, and to demonstrate how texture and performance in James are hardly ever disentangleable from moral meaning, however uncategorical.[1]

Daisy Miller is an early work – the first, as is well known, to give James a reputation – but it brilliantly embodies what became one of the key principles of James's later writing, not least in *The Turn of the Screw*: the obsessive building of expressive shapes and words around an enigma that cannot yield itself to direct expression or to direct knowledge. There is nothing more distinctively Jamesian than this constructive mode that relies on multiple aspects, nuances, and, as it were, resonation rather than statement.[2] As a creative mode it is exploratory, sly, self-reflexive, contradictory, and full of disguises – an art of the fox rather than the hedgehog. The underlying view of reality it posits is one based on fluidity, provisionality, and the perpetual to-and-fro process between consciousness and the outside world rather than on any more static concept of a determining essence or single cause. Intellectually and formally, James does not begin with some encapsulatable core, then work outward. Rather, he begins with the facets and ramifying aspects of a situation or a character, slowly establishes relationships between them, and between them and the rest of their fictional context, then works inward by increasing suggestion. Whatever may be at the core is released only by indirection, and it irradiates the formal patterns he makes only through the force of implication, by prefiguring, by echo, by hint, and therefore, inevitably and properly, by symbol. The hypothesized core can be approached, and its provisional presence revealed, only by the formal relationships that begin to move around it and to press inward against it, insinuatingly, and even contradictorily. The shapes of art, and the similar shaping of the interpretative mind, draw truth into their dance, revealing its presence and, equally, its instability as they do so. Where the very different art of a George Eliot, say – her art of the hedgehog – begins and ends with the core, as a clearly governing prior idea, a generalizable evaluation, James is likely to end as shiftingly, as prismatically and texturally, as he began. He is likely to end on a suggestive play of words, rather than a summing-up: the "clever foreign lady" of *Daisy Miller*'s last phrase that tweaks the narrative, by a witty half-echo, all the way back to the second paragraph of its opening.

Playful in performance, tragic in content: this is the Jamesian mixture that accompanies so rewarding a complexity of narrative method. It also makes for the peculiar dynamics of this book's narration, its rhythmic use of images of approach and withdrawal; its use of gaps and silences, sometimes alternating with moments

36

of sudden volubility or concussiveness; its special use of space, particularly of landscape space; its devices of repetition, inversion, and allusion; its use of the pictorial to offset the purely verbal, and vice versa; its occasional defocusing "play" with the potentially focusing device of point of view; its planned, ironic juggling with stereotypes and conventions; and, in general, its refusal ever to allow narrative to settle, thereby preserving its dynamic, both local and general, down to the very last words.[3]

Take, for example, the narrative use made of Daisy's little brother, Randolph, in the first of the four chapters.[4] He provides the novella's first moment of dramatic crystallization after two long opening paragraphs (which I will examine shortly) of genially expansive panorama and retrospect. Everything about him, exactly unlike those first two paragraphs, is pointed and aggressive: his unnaturally "aged expression of countenance" and "sharp little features"; the "brilliant red" of his stockings and cravat, and his "bright, penetrating little eyes" (4); above all the sharp alpenstock he carries around, like an emblem of his nature and his narrative function, thrusting "lance-fashion" into everything near him. Even the sound of the words "knickerbockers" and "spindleshanks," as applied to him, gives an appropriate raw edge to his image, like his pronunciation (only too American, James implies) of the word "har-r-r-d." His precocious assertiveness and rough opinionatedness, as well as being immediately comic, even farcical, in themselves, also have a straightforwardly satirical – that is, judgmental – role to play in the story's thematic concerned with cultivation and uncultivation. That role is highlighted. But more elliptically, more texturally, the concussive entry of this particular "small boy" throws us back to two small boys already mentioned in the narrative, the panoramic reference in the first paragraph to the "little Polish boys walking about, held by the hand, with their governors," and the retrospective reference in the second paragraph to Winterbourne having been "put to school [in Geneva] as a boy" (3–4). Randolph, so ungoverned, so unheld by any hand, is a comic inversion of the first (the repetition of an adjacent allusion to German waiters looking like diplomats makes the link even clearer). And Winterbourne's ponderously articulated recognition that "he might have the honour of claiming [Randolph] as a fellow-countryman" confirms the mirror effect ironically latent in the earlier reference to boyhood, himself as schoolboy in Geneva. But Randolph has another function at this stage, one that relates to what I have already mentioned as the narration's rhythm of approach-and-withdrawal. He acts as Winterbourne's – and as the reader's – go-between in the important narrative matter of introducing Daisy. " 'Here comes my sister,' " Randolph cries – for the narrative, as for Winterbourne – " 'She's an American girl.' " And Winterbourne flagrantly uses Randolph's obstreperousness, his xenophobic outbursts, his kicking up of the gravel, as an excuse for presenting himself to Daisy. Much of the movement of *Daisy Miller* will take this form of "an American girl" "advancing" and "drawing near" along a path, observed, spoken to, and analyzed by Winterbourne – then retreating or flouncing off, or otherwise forced out of the narrative foreground by Winterbourne's own excluding or banishing point of view. The use of Randolph as an introductory and introducing third party is to set his own juvenile "lance-like" forwardness as a foil to his sister's altogether different – more blurred, more suggestive – presentation of herself. Randolph and Randolph's voice never retreat, contain no mystery, are never defeated. His movement is comically outward. In introducing his sister, he is introducing his narrative opposite. And it is characteristic that a tale about the inadequacies of stereotypes and verbal tags, and the problem of ever giving a valid name to a personal identity, should show Randolph distributing national stereotypes and individual names as unequivocally and percussively as he kicks up gravel or stabs flower beds with his alpenstock: first, "American candy," "an American boy," "American men," "an American girl," then, with a rattle, "Randolph C. Miller," "Daisy Miller," "Annie P. Miller," "Ezra B. Miller," and, as his last stab, "Schenectady."

If Randolph in the opening pages offers a revealing instance of James's use of dynamic-by-contrast – introducing his central enigma of Daisy, and of any human identity, by a confident barrage of names and by the hard-edged unambiguity in a child's rude behavior – it is worth noting, too, that this introduction takes place in a chosen space, and after two significantly variable, even wavering, first paragraphs: the whole, Randolph, Winterbourne, Daisy, and the Jamesian stylistic approach forming a complex kinetic typical of the narrative to come. The opening paragraph, for example, sets up an extraordinarily varying rhythm of direction and attention. As soon as the opening sentence has drawn us firmly toward precision ("the little town," "Vevey," "Switzerland," and the intimately emphasizing "particularly" to individualize the one special hotel), the very next sentence swerves off into generality ("many hotels," "the business of the place"), then back into the particular ("a remarkably blue lake," where "remarkably" echoes the effect and style of "particularly" in the previous sentence), and off again into the grandly collective ("behoves every tourist to visit"). The detailed variety of types of hotels in Vevey (from "grand hotel" to "pension") is succeeded by the "one" hotel that concerns us, only for the narrative voice to sweep us off immediately into analogous images and echoes of far-off America where we are now "transported in fancy." The actual naming of Vevey's "particularly comfortable hotel" as the "Trois Couronnes" is achieved only within the context of incongruous American names, "Ocean House" (Newport) and "Congress Hall" (Saratoga). When the paragraph concludes by denying the American analogy, it does so by giving determining details of the Trois Couronnes that evoke not so much its Swissness as its cosmopolitanness: its German, Russian, and Polish associations. The Dents du Midi and the Castle of Chillon at the end are given as imaginative emblems of height and picturesqueness at least as much as names that specify and localize. The whole paragraph plays with our responses and expectations, and thereby leads us a dance – very gently, very wittily, but a dance nonetheless. Our imaginations, even before the appearance of Daisy at the core of the dance, are being appropriately attuned to a dynamic of approach and withdrawal, definition and blur, near and far, assertion and cancellation.

The dance also has its caller, its narrating voice.[5] The sense of this narrating presence is implied in that first paragraph's use of "particularly comfortable" and "remarkably blue" – both distinctly personal inflections – and also in the companionable phrase, "You receive an impression."[6] But the Jamesian device of playing with a self-revealing narrative point of view is fully released only in the second paragraph, immediately before the arrival of little Randolph. That arrival in its turn brings about a quick dramatization, a sinking of the point of view within Winterbourne himself, where it will remain, with only several exceptions, as the dominant mode of the tale's telling. The sudden appearance of a flagrantly narrating "I" in the second paragraph – the pronoun appears four times – is worth noting, for though James is very sparing in his use of the narrative "I" in the rest of the tale, his use of it here is a clue to certain more implicit narrative doublings and hesitations to come.[7]

When the narrator says, "I hardly know whether it was the analogies or the differences [between the Hotel des Trois Couronnes and certain American hotels] that were uppermost in the mind of a young American" (3–4), the effect is at once to open up a significant space in the narrative between telling voice and imaged character. Quizzically, playfully, James creates a gap between the "I" who draws attention to the mention of certain objects and the "young American," Winterbourne, who is observing them. The reader's stance becomes complicated by such playfulness. The emphasized gap between narrating voice and projected character, between the quasi-Jamesian "I" and "Winterbourne," is even confirmed by the arch phrase, "they must have seemed to him charming": that is, "he out there, for whom I am not really responsible, can safely be presumed to have felt the charm of these things." This momentary hiatus seems to me to work in two beautifully contradictory directions at once. First, the device confers a would-be objective status on Winterbourne, suggests his independence of the narrating "I," and thereby validates the mimetic and illusion-making function of the narration. If the "I" is not the total authority for everything it suggests is happening inside the character, then fiction is indeed miraculously approaching the condition of the real. But second, by drawing our attention to the "I," and thereby foregrounding the whole process – I emphasize "process" – of character making and story spinning, the device also denies approaching the condition of the real, and instead alerts us to the aesthetic ploy, and play, of all that is being said. The narrative voice goes on, "When his enemies spoke of him they said – but, after all, he had no enemies." And again, "Very few Americans – indeed I think none – had ever seen this lady" (4). In each of these minute hesitations of the narrating voice we have the same contradictory swerves: one in the direction of omniscience, one in the direction of dubiety. When a narrating voice (no matter how lightly, how chattily) pauses for a moment to question the very bases of its own knowledge concerning the fictional images it is inventing, we have, I suggest, a simultaneous enhancement of the otherness and independent reality of these images – involving something like momentary self-loss on the reader's part – and, on the contrary, an invitation to join with the fullest self-awareness in the subjective play of the text's antimimetic word spinning.[8]

Into this zone of epistemological sportiveness, this significant to-and-fro of subtle tale beginning, is made to step the young lady who will prove to be the catalyst of all such indecision. The first sight of her, typically, is of someone at the end of a pathway, advancing. And equally typically – in terms of technique as well as of moral and psychological theme – at the other end of the path is the observer, Winterbourne, itemizing the appearance of the approaching Daisy and categorizing her as an object of judgment. His categorical thinking ranges from "How pretty they are!" (note the depersonalizing plural of this, his first chosen category) to "a coquette," to "simply a pretty girl from New York State," to "an audacious, an unscrupulous young person," to "only a pretty American flirt" (this last being the formula he is "almost grateful" to settle on at this early stage). But as well as the clear concern of the narrative to demonstrate Winterbourne's almost obsessive (and self-defensive) need to find a formulaic judgment by which he can cope with the sexual and social phenomenon of Daisy, there is at the other end of his linear path of perception an interesting continuation of the narrative's opening rhythm of near and far that subtly undercuts Winterbourne's linearity of mind. In particular, the far is evoked by references – sometimes casual, sometimes emphasized – to the view of Lake Geneva from the hotel garden and of the Alps beyond: that panorama of "blue lake" and "snowy crest" which the opening paragraph alerted us to. When Daisy has for the first time "drawn near," and Winterbourne has itemized her "white muslin," her "hundred frills," "knots of pale-coloured

41

ribbon," and even, more minutely, the "deep border of embroidery" on her parasol, she pauses, contrastingly, "near the parapet of the garden, which overlooked the lake." When his self-conscious itemizing, his analytic noting of favorable "conditions" – "a pretty American girl coming and standing in front of you in a garden" – leads him to speak to her for the first time, her silent response, her otherness, is also articulated in terms of the recessive dimension of landscape: "She then turned her head and looked over the parapet, at the lake and the opposite mountains" (6). Daisy repeats her glance at the prospect when Randolph's little-brotherly brusqueness toward her succeeds Winterbourne's indecorous directness – only for the narrative quirkily to reverse their two roles for a moment. Daisy inspects her dress and smooths her ribbons – the near – while Winterbourne in the same sentence risks commenting on the beauty of the view – the far. When she turns her eyes full on Winterbourne, he gets "the benefit of her glance" (hitherto reserved mostly for what is distant, and enriched by it), while, again in the same sentence, he "pointed out some of the objects of interest in the view" (what is seen there by his itemizing mind, hitherto reserved for what is near). To complete the reversals and unexpected interweavings that articulate some of the alluring strangeness of the encounter, and of Daisy, her eyes look straight into Winterbourne's, then wander over the garden, look at the passers-by, and finally – where they began – at "the beautiful view": a comprehensiveness of survey, and a promise, entirely without commitment. If Daisy's behavior and words primarily tantalize Winterbourne in psychological terms – and his almost-governing point of view, in narrative terms, is by now established – these tiny destabilizing details of her eyes, and of the implied depths and distances behind them, work perfectly as a reiteration of the narration's local texture.

The physical space created in this first of the tale's four chapters – garden, parapet, bench, distant lake, and mountains – functions in at least three ways. Mimetically, it gives us a required sense of real place and three-dimensional movement: characters acting in a perspective of the ordinary world. Textually and linguistically, it is a variable gap: a stimulating play of contradictory possibilities, analogous to the plot's more explicit thematic. And symbolically, it images that thematic quite closely in its suggestion that Daisy's personality recedes beyond our direct knowing, into a distant area of enigma, yet can disconcertingly impinge on us directly, closely, incongruously: a glance as far as a mountain, or as close, and as crudely mundane, as a ribbon, a social gaucheness, a smile. Pertinent to this third, symbolic, application of space in the narrative is the use made of two of Daisy's possessions: her parasol (with its embroidered border) and her fan. These items are not just given a tactfully symbolic role to play – conventionally symbolic of female mystery and enigmatic allure – but they relate intimately to the images of view-watching and view-concealing that accrete quite densely in the narrative, and provide one of its richest pulses of linear (as well as of contrapuntal) dynamic.

The parasol is one of the first things we note about Daisy, on the morning of her encounter with Winterbourne: "She was bareheaded; but she balanced in her hand a large parasol, with a deep border of embroidery; and she was strikingly, admirably pretty" (5–6). In that sentence we see in the first clause Daisy's self-exposure (and simplicity); in the next clause, on the contrary, how she protects, and also projects, herself (even the word "balanced" turns holding the parasol into an unsimple theatrical gesture that is both considered and harmonizing, ostentatious and all-blending); and in the last clause, both as a revelation and a summation, a balance, of the previous play of opposites, we see how Winterbourne takes in her full attractiveness. The parasol is mentioned again at the moment when little Randolph and his alpenstock are at last got rid of, and Winterbourne can be alone with Daisy for the first time. The transition toward intimacy (of a kind) is ushered in by Daisy, seated next to him, "lowering her parasol and looking at the embroidered border" (8) – a double gesture that seems to combine the frank acceptance of closeness, a decorative ("embroidered") coquettishness, and a certain modest, eye-lowering self-consciousness. The poetic parasol is then transformed, slightly comically and vulgarly, into a mere instrument with which to point out, in a gesture worthy of Randolph himself, "that old castle," the Chateau de Chillon, that Daisy wants to visit. And in the penultimate sentence of chapter 1 the parasol marks Daisy's exit as it marked her entrance – "she gave him a smile

43

and turned away. She put up her parasol and walked back to the inn beside Eugenio. Winterbourne stood looking after her" (12) – but this time with the added theatricality for Winterbourne, left at the end of the path that stretches between them, of a new sense of being personally excluded and of having experienced a taunt to his irritated faculty of judgment.

After the totally different and concussive tone of the conversation between Winterbourne and Mrs. Costello that opens chapter 2, in which the faculty of judgment is translated (and vocalized) into the distinctly sharp dialectic of their aunt-and-nephew talk, Daisy is reintroduced by her evening equivalent of the parasol, her fan, and by new and quite contrasted epithets of poetry and even extravagance that see Mrs. Costello's language of categorical judgment firmly off the scene: "He found her that evening in the garden, wandering about in the warm starlight, like an indolent sylph, and swinging to and fro the largest fan he had ever beheld" (15). As though from behind the protection of her fan, from some shadowed depth of her personality, Daisy responds with her first pain to the judgmental world that now threatens to exclude her (in this perpetually veering tale Daisy is both excluded and one who excludes).[9] In a beautiful anticipation of one of the most moving of the glances-from-a-distance she bestows on Winterbourne – the very last between them, in the fatal "thick gloom" of the Colosseum – she now twice stares silently at him through the darkness as, embarrassed, he explains that his aunt, Mrs. Costello, declines to know her: "The young girl looked at him through the dusk," and "Miss Daisy Miller stopped and stood looking at him. Her prettiness was still visible in the darkness; she was opening and closing her enormous fan" (16). There is a particularly rich cluster of associations at this point. There is the association of the fan with darkness (real, but also symbolic in two opposite directions: the dark inner self, and the endless receding dark landscape); the association with her conventional feminine prettiness; the association with her never-quite-articulated inner nature (which needs the language of the fan's movement); and there is also a sudden slight depersonalization brought about by the stress of the moment ("the young girl," "Miss Daisy Miller") and now transferred to the impersonal gesturing of the fan. All this is consummately done, and, as always, with the lightest of touches. To confirm these suggestions, fan, eyes, and landscape space are at once brought together into another of those quickly evocative groupings of words by which James discreetly but poetically energizes the movement of his narrative, and for which "warm starlight" and "indolent sylph" have just prepared us. Daisy, in her pain and self-defensiveness, looks away into the distance, from the "parapet" that we are reminded overlooks "the starlit lake" with the "vague sheen upon its surface." It is exactly like the lowering and raising of the parasol, and the opening and closing of the fan. Daisy hides her hurt behind the fan-like gesture of her averted gaze and with a "little laugh," and in doing so looks at the "dimly seen mountain forms" that comprise the whole "mysterious prospect." In that resonant phrase, "mysterious prospect," set in the same sentence as Daisy's rather rattling and very close-at-hand "little laugh," coming so quickly after the mundane arguing voices of Mrs. Costello and Winterbourne, we have a striking – and very touching – instance of this narration's finesse in expressive variation.

The gesturing of the fan and the looks from behind the fan appear twice more in chapter 2, transformed into pure capriciousness and mild aggression, as Daisy, smiling, eyes gleaming, taunts the rigid Winterbourne into offering to take her out, scandalously, in a rowing boat at night: "Daisy turned away from Winterbourne, looking at him, smiling and fanning herself. 'Good night,' she said; 'I hope you are disappointed, or disgusted, or something!' " (21). The parasol – tightly folded, however, and unused by either its bearer or by the narrative – accompanies Daisy and Winterbourne two days later on their trip to Chillon. In Rome, two-thirds of the way through the whole narrative, the parasol makes its final and perhaps most effective appearance, in structural terms, beautifully linking the Swiss and Roman episodes, and serving also to concentrate the final and notably fast movement of the story by prefiguring the climactic scene in the Colosseum only about ten pages later. In each of the two pivotal scenes in question – the first in the Pincian Garden, the second in the Colosseum (where the parasol does not actually appear, but in our memory completely affects our reading of the scene's imagery and movement) – we encounter a characteristic complex of linear thrust, novelty, development, and of retrospective stasis, repetition, entrapment; of invitation to progress undercut by paralysis or retreat; of observation and potential vision cut short by the withdrawal of light; and of narrative itself, consciously doubling back on itself, briefly enacting the fictional dance and fate of its protagonists.

The Pincian Garden episode occupies the second half of chapter 3 of the novella; the first half consists mainly of the theatrically handled scene of Winterbourne meeting Daisy, her mother, and Randolph in Mrs. Walker's rooms, preceded briefly by Mrs. Costello's introductory account to her nephew of Daisy in Rome. The narrative mode in that first half has been essentially one of comedy-of-manners dialogue in drawing rooms, of interacting voices, gestures, and attitudes, with comic concussion from Randolph and Mrs. Miller, and its dominant purport has been the intensification of the process of assessment, categorization, and judgment (of Daisy by Winterbourne and, independently of Winterbourne, by the reader). Even when Daisy, so challengingly and so recklessly, walks out of Mrs. Walker's room with Winterbourne to meet Giovanelli on the Pincio, the pictorial element is kept surprisingly minimal: a brief reference to "the beautiful garden," to good weather, to "the slow-moving, idly gazing Roman crowd," to Giovanelli's rakish hat, monocle, and nosegay. Withholding the pictorial, in so potentially, indeed so overwhelmingly pictorial a setting, is extremely effective as a rhythmic device that in the end catalyzes revelation. Even Daisy, not usually sensitive to such opportunities, is allowed to tantalize us, and to remind us of what is being withheld, by saying to Winterbourne, "We had better go straight to that place in front – where you look at the view." On the word "view," the reader already begins to detect the possible echo of Vevey, but still has to wait for many pages before the narrative suddenly, at the very end of the episode, releases everything that has been withheld – with a parapet, a parasol, and a panoramic sunset. Through the Pincian Gardens excursion, right up to that last paragraph, the narration pens us almost claustrophobically into dialogue: Daisy's prattle, Winterbourne's objections to Giovanelli, Mrs. Walker's urgent moral remonstrations to Daisy from the authoritative position of her carriage, Winterbourne's and Mrs.

Walker's subsequent strained debate in the same carriage. The sudden switch from dialectic, combative, judging voices to the extravagantly pictorial concluding paragraph is an entirely characteristic piece of alternation in mode. The piling up of pressure-within-discussion, usually discussion *à deux*, reinforced by the tight focus on Winterbourne's equally claustrophobic psychological reactions, effectively highlights the more pictorial, more poetically suggestive, and certainly more enlarging units of narration when they occur. The rhythm set up – or rather, the overall narrative rhythm which this device confirms – is one of constriction against release, discriminated words against potent images, social discourse against poetry, judgment against imaginative sympathy: the basic duality of the whole case of Daisy Miller.

The restrictive carriage, the decorously enveloping carriage rug, and above all the domineering voice of Mrs. Walker's earnest conscience, are replaced, in the last paragraph, by a quite different local rhythm of approach and withdrawal, promised intimacy and exclusion, even of self-exclusion, of closeness and distance. The "view," long promised to us, is about to be unveiled at last, both literally and metaphorically. The word "parapet" is given twice, and the words "overlooks" and "overhangs." Daisy and Giovanelli are walking together toward the parapet; Winterbourne, descended from Mrs. Walker's carriage, observes them unmoving. Mrs. Walker's silent look at Winterbourne, as she drives off "majestically" in her victoria, is an ironic inversion of the silent looks he received from Daisy at Vevey, and is soon to receive again from her, in the Colosseum ("looked at him a moment" is the very phrase used here, of Mrs. Walker, and in the Colosseum, of Daisy). The "look" is now of another kind: Winterbourne's defeated "look" at the other couple as they "look" out at the revealed prospect from the old wall of Rome: not now the prospect of "dimly-seen mountain forms" that were the metaphor at Vevey for all that might lie behind and within Daisy, but the equally evocative "great flat-topped pine-clusters of the Villa Borghese," and the "western sun" as it sends out "a brilliant shaft through a couple of cloud-bars." The prospect of richness available to Daisy and Giovanelli, and by implication available *through* Daisy, is at once shut off for the observer Winterbourne, too much Mrs. Walk-

47

er's protégé. Daisy's parasol is mentioned three times in the closing sentences. It is in the hands of Giovanelli, who momentarily seems to have established possessive rights to the owner whom it screens and whom it symbolizes. The movements are small, precise, and suggestive. "She came a little nearer and he held the parasol over her; then, still holding it, he let it rest upon her shoulder, so that both their heads were hidden from Winterbourne" (36). Behind the parasol the couple are not only sexually close together, and distant, because screened, from Winterbourne; they are also looking out over the wide prospect of universal light and Roman color which is similarly denied to him. The only movement left to Winterbourne, and to the narration at the end of this chapter of Roman arrival, encounter, and analysis, followed by its single moment of limitless pictorial expansion and by allusions (the parasol, the view, the look) that are both retrospective and premonitory, is one of retreat, emphasized by the subtly punctilious yet ambiguous phrasing that raises the possibility of a forward direction ("then he began to walk"), maintains it in suspense for a second ("But he walked –"), only to define it finally by a negation ("not towards the couple"). The concluding bathos of "the residence of his aunt, Mrs. Costello" – whose authoritarian critique of Daisy, even crisper than Mrs. Walker's, began the chapter some twelve pages earlier, and now closes its frame as tightly as a "residence" or as a carriage rug in a victoria – leaves Winterbourne more viewless than ever, and the visionary prospect of mingled sky and human intimacy more isolated, and therefore more intense, within a narration that so quickly and ironically doubles itself back into the categories, and toward the categorizing, of the social.

The parapet, the parasol, and the sunset view, among their other, mostly symbolic, functions, refer backward to Vevey at the beginning, and forward to the Colosseum, near the end, of the narrative. They thereby give what repetition in narrative so often gives, a contradictory combination of linearity, marked progressively by the recurrence of a developing motif, and of circularity, where recurrence gives a thematic perception of the preordained, the treadmill: *Daisy Miller* as a tale of youth, possibility, encounter, prospect, and desire, against the very same tale as one of fated disappointment, error, moral paralysis, and death.[10] In the Colosseum at midnight, where death and closure are waiting, there is no parasol, but there are a variety of prospects, and a shadow that, exactly like a parasol, screens Daisy from exposure, suggests a taunting intimacy, shuts out Winterbourne, and has an associative resonance – a deadly, abstracting resonance – of what lies potently behind it, a distance of space and of time. In a half-echo of the "vague sheen" on Lake Geneva and the "dimly-seen mountain forms" of Winterbourne's encounter with Daisy at night in Vevey, we have the "vaguely-lighted monuments of the Forum." Confronted by the Alps, Winterbourne was more the connoisseur and pedagogue than the poet, pointing out to Daisy "the objects of interest." And now (repetitiously, caught in the treadmill of self), he enters the Colosseum "as a lover of the picturesque," thinking, Baedekerlike, that it "would be well worth a glance," and, prudential as always, interrupting his brief effusion into Byronic quotation by remembering the nocturnal risk of malaria. Almost as soon as he has entered the place of poetic "prospect" ("pale moonshine," "clear and silent arena," "gigantic circus," "luminous dusk") he is bent on "a hasty retreat." If the parasol, in the two earlier episodes, was associated equally with enticement and exclusion, here we have a complete development of that pattern of fascinated approach and repudiatory retreat, enacting in compressed and connotative image form what so much surrounding drawing room dialogue and psychological appraisal has generated in its more discursive dialectic.

Daisy, as ever, is at the very center of things, but now associated, by the central cross at the feet of which she and Giovanelli are seated in shadowed intimacy, with the Christian past, with the idea of sacrifice and of victimization. The associations are made lightly, even humorously, in Daisy's and Giovanelli's bantering allusions to lions, Christian martyrs, and being eaten alive. But the qualifying humor is only a perfect and characteristically Jamesian stabilizer of such rich associations, not in the least a demolisher of them. Winterbourne is irredeemably – though perhaps inevitably, humanly, and averagely – at the far end of the "path" from such a center. The shadow over Daisy, and over the central cross, shuts him out forever; the shadow has the distinctly new suggestion of her coming death to add to (even to contradict, tragically) the earlier association of a "mysterious prospect" in her personality and life. Winterbourne, ironically, is in the light: a daytime survivor, a dweller in a daytime "residence," and unable to "read" either darkness or Daisy. Light, which might be a mode of vision for Winterbourne, becomes only a mode of exposure. The couple in the dark watch the man in the light hesitate and turn disapprovingly away from them: it is Winterbourne, not Daisy, who can therefore be "read." In a touch that beautifully brings together, first, the categorizing, moral discourse of the scenes of social comedy and debate, and, second, the poetic, imagistic discourse of such heightened moments as those at the Pincio and at the Colosseum, Winterbourne is relieved, indeed exultant, to discover a moral and linguistic cliché – a dead and deadeningly inadequate concept – that will shield him from further dubiety or exposure to the prospect of Daisy: "She was a young lady whom a gentleman need no longer be at pains to respect" (46).[11] This so-called answer to the riddle of Daisy, which has come straight from the language and mental fixity of the drawing room – Mrs. Costello's, Mrs. Walker's – flashes upon Winterbourne in "a sudden illumination." The ironic conflation of the two worlds of discourse is perfect. The answering of riddles is intrinsic to the Costello-Walker categorization of human behavior, whereas "illumination" is, or ought to be, intrinsic to the poetic chiaroscuro of the Colosseum. In that world of "pale moonshine," Winterbourne, who now stands revealed to others, is yet blind in himself. His mental "illumination," as a mere riddle solver, is patently delusive and insufficient. Some riddles are not for solving – only, perhaps, for loving.

Winterbourne starts to go forward toward Daisy, then stops and goes back, his life of hesitation thus choreographed for us, as so often, in the very movement of the narrative. Then at Daisy's expostulation he goes forward again, then leaves at last in Daisy's company. Daisy's glance, too, repeats something of its old dance of sexual assertiveness alternating with withdrawal into an area, an inner prospect, of infinite private reserve. "Daisy, lovely in the flattering moonlight, looked at him a moment" – even the willful mention of "flattering" is there to deflect any certainty. Can such a to-and-fro narration allow one to be sure even about loveliness? The very last exchange between Winterbourne and Daisy, as she prepares to leave with Giovanelli in her carriage, is a characteristic affair of spoken language undercut by silence and, therefore, by space.[12] Winterbourne's laughing words are harshly contemptuous: "I believe that it makes very little difference whether you are engaged or not!" Daisy's reply is a rhythmic and syntactic echo of Winterbourne's, the two forming an ironic, because fatally antithetic, couplet: " 'I don't care,' said Daisy, in a little strange tone, 'whether I have Roman fever or not!' " (47–8). The enforced grammatical echo makes the emotional point: without Winterbourne's jealous concern and affection she has no interest left in life. One follows the other, as closely as an echo. Between the two lines of dialogue – his dismissive of any affection for Daisy, hers, in implied consequence, despairing and self-abandoning – her eyes for the second time fix on him, wordlessly, "through the thick gloom of the archway." Whatever is in her glance, as well as whatever is beneath her words (beyond even the hint of their "little strange tone"), is articulated only by being withheld – and by being extrapolated poetically and eloquently in the suggestive sense of place and view, of archway, of Colosseum, of history and suffering, of dark and light, of gloomy finality that the narration so subtly invokes. Daisy's last line of direct dialogue is the narrative's one confession of love. In a tale about incommunication, and about the distance-beyond-words of one young woman's growing inner world of feeling, it comes to us appropriately through the indirections of silence and of richly associative imagery, quite counter to the surface brusqueness and briskness of language.

For a narration that makes a point of the imperfections of social language – in particular the language that judges personality and behavior – and of categorical analysis as a deeply inadequate mode of knowing another person, it is notable how much of *Daisy Miller* is taken up by demonstrations of exactly these two modes of discourse – interrupted, and therefore ironized, by moments of the very different stylistic resonances I have described. Characteristic of Winterbourne's play of consciousness, for example, and also of the tone of omniscient narratorial comment on his type of consciousness, is this, in chapter 1: "He had a great relish for feminine beauty; he was addicted to observing and analysing it; and as regards this young lady's face he made several observations" (7). This is followed by such telltale forensic phrases as "Winterbourne mentally accused it," "He thought it very possible," "he was sure," "It might have been said of this unknown young lady that...," "to say such things seemed a kind of demonstrative evidence of a certain laxity of deportment," and "she was only a pretty American flirt. Winterbourne was almost grateful for having found the formula that applied to Miss Daisy Miller" (10). Other summary formulae for Daisy (and others) include the following, all presented under a glistening irony that nevertheless never quite destroys the possibility of their partial validity within the terms of that same hardedged, intellectual, social register: "very common" (from Mrs. Costello), "rather wild" (from Winterbourne), "completely uncultivated" (Winterbourne), "a dreadful girl" (Mrs. Costello), "dreadful people" and "hopelessly vulgar" (Mrs. Costello), "not a gentleman" (Winterbourne, of Giovanelli), "[not] a perfectly well-conducted young lady" (Winterbourne), "a very reckless girl" (Mrs. Walker), "naturally indelicate" (Mrs. Walker), "a very light young person" (Winterbourne), "assigned to a vulgar place among the categories of disorder" (Winterbourne listening to Mrs. Costello on Daisy), "a young person of the reckless class" (Winterbourne), and finally, as we have seen, "a young lady whom a gentleman need no longer be at pains to respect" (Winterbourne). This makes for a perfect barrage of would-be definitive epithets that by their very excess ("a pretty American flirt" occurs five times) undermine their own definitiveness, and end up by spreading doubt – an untouched space at the core – exactly where they purport to impose a finally clarifying and reifying category.

Winterbourne's continually categorizing and tabulating attention to his own reactions to Daisy, added to the dialogue's cleverly theatrical deployment of question-and-answer, or of table-tennis-like persiflage, gives an almost Socratic pointedness to many of the cut-and-thrust discussions or consciousness-analyzing scenes in the narrative. The reader takes pleasure in the wit that governs many of these exchanges – those between Winterbourne and Mrs. Costello, for example, which have something of a Wildean high style of polite abrasiveness – and in the self-advertising cleverness of the omniscient narrator's comments ("Mrs. Costello was a widow with a fortune; a person of much distinction, who frequently intimated that, if she were not so dreadfully liable to sick-headaches, she would probably have left a deeper impress upon her time" [13]). The narration thus necessarily connives at the categorizing, rationalistic style it ultimately disparages, and which it often disparages simultaneously with its self-pleasing conniving, as in this example at the beginning of chapter 4: "Mrs. Walker was one of those American ladies who, while residing abroad, make a point, in their own phrase, of studying European society; and she had on this occasion collected several specimens of her diversely-born fellow-mortals to serve, as it were, as text-books" (36). The narrating voice is clearly satirical of Mrs. Walker and her activities, but despite such self-distancing ploys as "in their own phrase" and "as it were," there is the sense of an epigrammatic and specimen-collecting stylist behind the very voice that satirizes specimen-collecting and the formulaic cast of the epigram. There is nothing self-cancelling about this contradiction: it is something of a Jamesian hallmark. Indeed, the story's typically Jamesian thematic concern to show the complexity of social living and the contradictoriness of the social individual's impulses is only expressed better for the narration's pervasive involvement in that same paradoxicality, the paradoxicality intrinsic to all human consciousness, as between the intelligence (which creates categories) and the imagination (which inhabits images).

This narration challenges its own various modes at all points: self-challenging, self-testing being one of the keynotes of James's fiction. The discursive and the lyrical, the comedy of manners and the prose-poem, are scrupulously played off against one another throughout – even in a tiny example like this, early in chapter 3: "[Mrs. Walker] was a very accomplished woman and she lived in the Via Gregoriana. Winterbourne found her in a little crimson drawing-room, on a third floor; the room was filled with southern sunshine. He had not been there for ten minutes when the servant came in, announcing 'Madame Mila!' " (26). The sophisticated knowingness in the structuring of that first sentence (merely to live in the Via Gregoriana is clearly sufficient proof of being accomplished), and the quick, comic, theatrical business of Mrs. Miller's entrance, together form the dominant note of the episode but are bisected by that completely arbitrary evocation of Roman color and light, the two referred to separately but combining incandescently in the mind's eye. It seems to tell us nothing different about Mrs. Walker's taste: southern crimson sensuousness hardly fits her. The minute intrusion of another (incandescent) world, and of another style (the imagination inhabiting its image), reminds us of all that is not in her register, or in her social categories: something that is always hinted at in the depths of Winterbourne's otherwise too-accomplished perceptions, and, by association, is just about to invade and disturb the drawing room (and those perceptions) in the uncategorizable shape of Daisy herself, following her mother.

The use of the pictorial to contradict the purely verbal, and, in particular, of landscape space to irradiate and change the logical and dialectical, is nowhere employed more brilliantly than in the penultimate meeting of Winterbourne and Daisy, which occurs halfway through chapter 4 in the Palace of the Caesars. In the overall developing structure of the narrative, as well as texturally and locally, the paragraph is rich and crucial. Its climactic phrase seems to be "mysterious interfusion," a small but significant echo of that earlier "mysterious prospect" of "dimly-seen mountain forms" by night at Vevey (chapter 2). If much of the tale's thematic interest can be seen as focused on division and breakdown, here we have one brief, poised instant where union – mysterious fusion – seems to be possible; and possible not by intent or by intelligence or by rational cognition, but by "mystery." The ruined Palace is a "beautiful abode of flowering desolation" – these two last words forming a fine and tense oxymoron. Desolation is momentarily balanced by its flowering opposite, and the "rugged surface" of a dead, Imperial city is "muffled with tender verdure": "muffled," by a wonderful economy, suggesting not only the silencing of the sound of present footsteps but also the now-silenced clamor of the historical past (the chattering drawing rooms, as it were, of the old Roman lawgivers on the Palatine). The sight of Daisy walking on the marble ruins, with their "monumental inscriptions," makes Winterbourne see Rome as lovelier than ever before, and as redeemed from all in its history that threatens "interfusion." Daisy's youth – "tender verdure" (her name, too, is a flower) – is part of what "muffles" the harsh Imperial associations, especially the hint of authoritarian busyness and control in those "inscriptions," which also suggest the categorizing, noisy, and prescriptive word making of such almost-Roman matrons as Mrs. Costello and Mrs. Walker, and their proclamatory and discriminating narrative mode, stilled for this one paragraph. In the preceding paragraph, by perfect and extreme contrast, that mode has been at its most pointed, with Winterbourne's analysis of Daisy's career carried to its most abstract (even in vocabulary), and its most self-vexing in effect: "he was angry at finding himself reduced to chopping logic about this young lady; he was vexed at his want of instinctive certitude" (43). From his usual treadmill of the judgmental, ethical mind, Winterbourne is here transported, in a dazzling switch of direction, to the peaceful "space" that the imagery of place creates. Instead of "logic" and self-scrutiny there is the "harmony" of balanced associations, balanced around the core, the center, of Daisy strolling on the transformed ruins of Imperial Rome.[13]

The one extraordinary sentence that ends with "mysterious interfusion" comprehends many things: "He stood looking off at the enchanting harmony of line and colour that remotely encircles the city, inhaling the softly humid odours and feeling the freshness of the year and the antiquity of the place reaffirm themselves in mysterious interfusion" (44). This embraces the aesthetic ("line and colour"), the historical ("the antiquity of the place"), sight, smell ("odours"), and touch ("softly humid"), youth and age ("freshness" and "antiquity"), a city, an observer, and a distant circle that surrounds the city, a widening, expanding image of wholeness and consummation, to which the conglomerate syllables and "s" sounds of "mysterious interfusion" make a suitably poetic final cadence. And in the unexpected verb near the end of the sentence, "reaffirm," we have the idea of repetition in its most creative, its least treadmill, form, signifying that this moment of intense vision is not casual, being an affirmation, and is not finite, being a returning *re*-affirmation.

It is of the essence of this story's narrative dynamic that even such a profound moment of plenitude – the Romantic vision of wholeness, the "great good place" that haunts and eludes so many of James's fictional protagonists, as it now eludes Winterbourne – should be rhetorically so understated, and above all that it should not last.

In the very same paragraph the narration abruptly diverges – even dwindles – into the very workaday, very categorical mode of Winterbourne making yet another "observation," and Giovanelli caught in yet another wittily "placing" epigram. Daisy's and Winterbourne's argumentative voices fill up the momentary space of the Palace of the Caesars with their social and sexual abrasiveness, their all-too-human words that reach out hopelessly toward one another and always fall back, in bathos and half-comprehension, far removed from any mysterious or even mundane interfusion.

Except that one echo – in this narration of subtle echoes and doublings – remains. Daisy's death is conveyed in the laconic, carefully unpoetic language, the social register, of the worldly observer: "A week after this the poor girl died; it had been a terrible case of the fever" (49). But in the one pregnantly allusive sentence that follows, the poetic (and personal) lost promise of both the Pincian Garden and the Palace of the Caesars is suddenly and briefly interjected into the merely urbane: "Daisy's grave was in the little Protestant cemetery, in an angle of the wall of Imperial Rome, beneath the cypresses and the thick spring-flowers." The "wall" of Imperial Rome directs us back, quite dizzyingly, to the same wall of Rome from the parapet of which Daisy, with Giovanelli, had taken in the life-filled prospect of the sunlight over the Pincian Garden. And "Imperial Rome" qualified by "spring-flowers" echoes the "tender verdure" that muffled the Palatine and softened, with its youthfulness, the "monumental inscriptions" at the Palace of the Caesars. To evoke so concentratedly, yet so lightly, those two episodes of richness and expectation, transposed here to the utterly opposed moment of the burial of all such hopes, not only displays great narrative suppleness and imagistic allusiveness. In its laconic flashing together of remembered promise and present loss, it is a classic (in theatrical terms, a fifth-act) distillation of tragic insight.[14]

At the graveside, Winterbourne is left "staring at the raw protuberance among the April daisies."[15] The "spring-flowers," the "tender verdure," and "Daisy" herself have been counterchecked by the obtrusion of death. The gaping monosyllable, "raw," perfectly complements the bulging, awkward consonants (yet the strangely accompanying abstraction) of "protuberance." That phrase is a poet's – or, rather, it lingers from the poetic mode persistent within a narration. But the final pulse of the narrative's dynamism leads back into the enduring prose world, the logic chopping of Mrs. Costello's closing polemic with Winterbourne: the witty mode of question-and-answer, dissection, yet of continuing verbal ambiguity. The narration slips back into the present tense of the tale's first paragraph – opening it up to the notion of continuation and unclosed irresolution.[16] But the allusion to Winterbourne "studying," and to his interest in a "clever foreign lady," contradictorily locks the door on change and openness by returning us verbally to the second paragraph, where he was doing just those things: caught, thus, in his eternal treadmill. Between these story making impulses of opening and closure, of liberating distance against restrictive category, between the imagination's opening "prospect" and the reason's concluding "study," between a certain "America" and a certain "Europe," the enigma of Daisy and her narrative has traced its dynamics: that is, between the ironically opposed poles of her story's double title, *Daisy Miller: A Study.*[17]

NOTES

1. Most thematic criticism of *Daisy Miller* – which, as I have said, seems to mean most criticism of *Daisy Miller* – has in the past emphasized the "international theme" aspect of the story, or, more recently, Winterbourne as a categorizing, life-fearing male, and even novelist-like center of consciousness. My own earlier thematic reading of the tale in *Henry James: The Drama of Fulfilment* (Oxford: Oxford University Press, 1975) compared it with the romantic-ironic mode of "Madame de Mauves," and saw it as "a tragicomedy of judgement and knowledge," with particular regard to Winterbourne's use of mechanistic formulae and stereotypes – its mingled medium of satire and pathos bearing a Chekhov-like vision "of a desired but always elusive ful-

filment to all human living, individual and collective; of mind and temperament striving for ultimate shape; of baffled lovers on their terraces, staring at a city or a sunset" (p. 28).

The most recent long study of the tale, by Millicent Bell, in her humanely argued *Meaning in Henry James* (Cambridge, Mass.: Harvard University Press, 1991), continues the "stereotype" and "formula" approach to Winterbourne, its "author-surrogate and anti-hero" (p. 49), who displays "recognizably *masculine* ways of looking at women" (p. 55), and who uses tritely subliterary concepts and language. Yet she too sees the narrative as an "interpretive contest" (p. 65) over the meaning of Daisy herself that remains ambiguous to the end. Bell at one point mentions that "the progress of the narrative, which follows the seesaw mental swings of Winterbourne, exhibits, already, that crab-wise narrative progress which will reach its full expression in *The Ambassadors*" (p. 49), but her main concern remains interpretation rather than process and texture.

2. Sergio Perosa, for one, writing with clarity about James as an "experimental" writer, sees narrative "multiplication of aspects" (the phrase is James's, from the preface to *The Awkward Age*) as one of the signs of James's drama-influenced novels of the later 1890s, and therefore of his emergent modernism (*Henry James and the Experimental Novel* [New York: New York University Press, 1983], *passim*). This is indisputable, but "experimentalism" could well be pushed right back to the beginning of James's career, in *The Europeans* as well as in *Daisy Miller* (both first published in 1878). See my own analysis of such experimental complexity of narrative movement in *The Europeans* in *Indirections of the Novel: James, Conrad, Forster* (Cambridge, England: Cambridge University Press, 1988, pp. 19–32).

3. Any analysis based on these narrative dynamics must clearly draw support and some of its strategies from the overwhelming emphasis over the last thirty years on the indeterminacy and "play" of literary texts that has come from structuralist, poststructuralist, deconstructionist, and reader-response theorizing – from the varied (and at times internecine) writings of figures like Barthes, Derrida, Iser, Genette, Todorov, Miller, Holland, Fish, and many others. But insofar as my own present essay is pragmatic and not theoretic or taxonomic (who could be taxonomic faced by Winterbourne's example?), and does not in the least approach the deconstructionist position that what a literary text primarily conveys is its own unreadability in terms of meaning, I can only quote here, as of possible relevance, James's own account of the ideal critic (which none of us can be). It is a daunting,

invigorating, unfashionable view, in particular, of the *instrumentality* of the critic, and it attributes to the act of criticism a twofold kinetic of approach and withdrawal, curiosity and patience, subjectivity and objectivity, self-projection and protean understanding, direction and giving that resembles the basic rhythms of *Daisy Miller* that I am trying to identify:

there is something sacrificial in [the critic's] function, inasmuch as he offers himself as a general touchstone. To lend himself, to project himself and steep himself, to feel and feel till he understands and to understand so well that he can say, to have perception at the pitch of passion and expression as embracing as the air, to be infinitely curious and incorrigibly patient, and yet plastic and inflammable and determinable, stooping to conquer and serving to direct – these are fine chances for an active mind, chances to add the idea of independent beauty to the conception of success. Just in proportion as he is sentient and restless, just in proportion as he reacts and reciprocates and penetrates, is the critic a valuable instrument; for in literature assuredly criticism *is* the critic, just as art is the artist. ("Criticism," *New Review*, 1891, reprinted in *Theory of Fiction: Henry James*, ed. James E. Miller [Lincoln: University of Nebraska Press, 1972], pp. 331–2)

4. I have taken as my text the widely reprinted 1879 Macmillan edition, the first book version supervised by James himself. Page references, where given, are to the reprint of this text in the Norton Critical Edition of *Tales of Henry James*, ed. Christof Wegelin (New York: Norton, 1984). Very brief quotations are not page referenced, and in view of the many available reprints reference is also made, where possible, to the appropriate chapter (the tale has four) or to the particular episode.

5. The venerable phrase "point of view," which I go on to use, has really not been superseded as a term for this aspect of narrative method, despite the rival claims of Gérard Genette's "focalization." For a recent clearheaded survey of the history of the concept, see "Points of View on Point of View," in Wallace Martin's useful *Recent Theories of Narrative* (Ithaca: Cornell University Press, 1986), pp. 130–51.

6. William Veeder might perhaps have classed these "personal inflections" as belonging to the early James's unsubtle use of stereotypical intensifiers – his quantitative and qualitative analysis of words like "remarkably" and "perfectly" in, say, *Roderick Hudson*, is very sobering (see his *Henry James—The Lessons of the Master* [Chicago: University of Chicago Press, 1975], pp. 20–53). However, when Veeder

goes on to analyze the "personal," that is, the distinctive and not merely cultural or stereotypical, elements in James's slightly later style – for example, in *Washington Square* and *Portrait of a Lady* – he brings out very effectively, if a little reluctantly, some of the same syntactical suggestiveness and successful rhetorical counterpointing that I find throughout *Daisy Miller* (a work he does not consider).

7. In the rest of the narrative, the narratorial "our" occurs once, in chap. 2 (21), and the narratorial "I" three times, once in chap. 3 (34) and twice in chap. 4 (40, 43). There are naturally several other indications of omniscience, but the focus on Winterbourne is remarkably consistent. Wayne Booth, however, exaggerates in considering the story's point of view under the general heading of "Authorial Silence"; he is surely unsubtle in concluding that James's consistent use of Winterbourne as an unreliable observer is in order to reduce the effect of pathos in Daisy: "Seen through his eyes she can hardly become emotionally important to us" (*The Rhetoric of Fiction* [Chicago: University of Chicago Press, 1961], pp. 282–4). Most of James's "silences" are very eloquent, and feeling for Daisy flows through them perfectly freely.

8. There is a pertinent and highly abstract account of this effect of "distanciation" based on the variable relation between the reader and his or her self-awareness by Paul Ricoeur, in *Interpretation Theory* (Fort Worth: Texas Christian University Press, 1976).

9. My point here, and the emphasis throughout my account, that Daisy is no mere passive or hopelessly naive victim of society's ostracism but has an at least implied inner world of growing self-awareness and a certain sensitivity, irony, and desire (often symbolized by gesture and by landscape), from which Winterbourne and the others find themselves excluded to their cost, comes up against the objection of James's own disclaimer, in a letter of 1880:

[Daisy] never took the measure really of the scandal she produced, and had no means of doing so: she was too ignorant, too irreflective, too little versed in the proportions of things. . . . to my perception she never really tried to take her revenge upon public opinion – to outrage it and irritate it. (*Henry James: Selected Letters*, ed. Leon Edel [Cambridge, Mass.: Harvard University Press, 1987], p. 170)

Against James's own words I can only adduce the adage, "Trust the tale, not the teller," and suggest that James in his letter is overcompensating for some nagging sense of having presented Daisy not critically enough and (as he acknowledged rather ruefully in the

preface over twenty-five years later) "quite inordinately and extravagantly, in poetical terms." See also note 17, below.

10. On this possible contradictory effect of repetition, compare the pos-
itive view of E. K. Brown: "To express what is both an order and a
mystery rhythmic processes, repetition with intricate variations, are
the most appropriate of idioms" (*Rhythm in the Novel* [Toronto: University of Toronto Press, 1950], p. 115), with Peter Brooks's more
apocalyptic and neo-Freudian view: "Repetition as return speaks as
a textual version of the death instinct, plotting the text, beyond the
seeming dominance of the pleasure principle, towards its proper end,
imaging this end as necessarily a time before the beginning" ("Repetition, Repression, and Return: *Great Expectations* and the Study of
Plot," *New Literary History* 11 [1979–80]: 503–26). For more on repetition see also J. Hillis Miller's far-from-apocalyptic *Fiction and Repetition: Seven English Novels* (Oxford: Oxford University Press, 1982);
and Paul Ricoeur, "Narrative Time," in *On Narrative*, ed. W. J. T.
Mitchell (Chicago: University of Chicago Press, 1981), pp. 165–86.

11. James's quite radical revisions of *Daisy Miller* for the New York Edition
of 1907–09, which are not directly relevant to my present purpose,
interestingly elaborate on the black-and-white motif at this point of
the narrative, changing the phrase just quoted to this: "She was a
young lady about the *shades* of whose perversity a foolish puzzled
gentleman need no longer trouble his head or his heart. That once
questionable quantity *had* no shades – it was a mere black little blot"
(New York Edition, reprinted [New York: Augustus Kelley, 1971],
vol. 18, p. 86). James also added that Daisy's words to Winterbourne
"fluttered and settled about him in the darkness like vague white
doves" (ibid., pp. 85–6). See Viola Dunbar, "The Revision of *Daisy
Miller*," *Modern Language Notes* 65 (1950): 311–17; and my note 16
below. See also Richard Hocks's comment on "shades" and "lightness
and darkness" in his *"Daisy Miller*, Backward into the Past: a Cen-
tennial Essay," *Henry James Review* 1 (1980): 176–7.

12. Nicola Bradbury writes well about the expressive use of silence in
James's later writing, in her *Henry James: The Later Novels* (Oxford:
Oxford University Press, 1979), pp. 13–35. On the role of silence and
silent gesture in *The Europeans*, see my *Indirections of the Novel: James,
Conrad, Forster* (Cambridge, England: Cambridge University Press,
1988), pp. 21–4.

13. James's image of some all-embracing mysterious harmony in which
contradictions might end pervades all his writing, both as a motif and
as a motivating desire, and makes one of his strongest points of

connection with Romanticism. For a full-scale treatment of the topic see Daniel Mark Fogel, *Henry James and the Structure of the Romantic Imagination* (Baton Rouge: Louisiana State University Press, 1981). For example: "A demonstration of the affinity of James's imagination for the Romantic dialectic of spiral return entails attention to two aspects of James's practice: his characteristic use of polarities and his inveterate (though sometimes thwarted) movement to synthesis" (ibid., p. 8).

14. Compare this account with Ruth Yeazell, who, somewhat overfavoring late-Jamesian complexity of language at the expense of early James, contrasts the power of the "dove" image for Milly Theale in *The Wings of the Dove* with what she sees as the lack of such richness in *Daisy Miller,* whose heroine was Milly's prototype: "The metaphor transforms Milly's death, bestows on it a significance that Daisy Miller's pathetic collapse never fully achieves" (*Language and Knowledge in the Late Novels of Henry James* [Chicago: University of Chicago Press, 1980], p. 56). Although not gainsaying the far greater range of *The Wings of the Dove,* my own reading of how James controls and expands the death of Daisy insists that it is far more than a "pathetic collapse."

15. Richard Hocks's is the most extravagant notation I know on the various emblematic associations of the name Daisy, all of which he sees as operative in the narrative – from the particular "North American daisy" to the "day's eye" to the "English daisy" (apparently also known, significantly in this case, as "bachelor's button") to the American slang word for "first-rate" (*"Daisy Miller,* Backward into the Past," 174). For myself, I am happy to settle for only one: a spring flower associated with freshness and innocence.

16. On the open-endedness of the Jamesian novel and others see Marianna Torgovnick, *Closure in the Novel* (Princeton: Princeton University Press, 1981); also, more generally, Frank Kermode, *The Sense of an Ending* (Oxford: Oxford University Press, 1966).

17. James deleted "A Study" from the title for the New York Edition, partly because he admitted whimsically in the preface he could not remember why he chose it – "[unless] perhaps after all the attached epithet was meant but as a deprecation, addressed to the reader, of any great critical hope of stirring scenes" – and partly because, looking back, he saw "A Study" as being incongruous in its "critical" sound with the actual "poetical terms" in which his "little exhibition ... quite inordinately and extravagantly" was carried out (*The Art of the Novel: Critical Prefaces by Henry James,* ed. R. P. Blackmur [New York:

Scribner's, 1934], pp. 268–9). The later loss of that trenchant oxymoron of the full original title is in my opinion not the only loss the story sustains under James's later half-disparagement and his late-manner revisions.

Winterbourne and the Doom of Manhood in *Daisy Miller*

ROBERT WEISBUCH

1

HENRY JAMES is like the modern jazz masters in this: He begins with the simplest romantic themes, then builds intricacies upon them until the once-clichés speak to all the subtle richness of social existence. With Daisy Miller and her reluctant suitor Frederick Winterbourne, the theme is no more than "opposites attract," and the trick is that one pole of that opposition is so constructed as to make the attraction deadly. "Stiff" Winterbourne brings doom to Daisy and a different doom to himself; through him, James tallies the evils of a misconstructed masculinity.

It's a multifaceted opposition between the failed lovers, but at base simple as motion through the world. Daisy Miller moves. She "goes on," "goes round," "goes too far," well over a hundred times in the text. "She goes on," a particular persecutor remarks, "from day to day, from hour to hour, as they did in the Golden Age."[1] No enthusiast of the dynamic, Mrs. Costello "can imagine nothing more vulgar." Too blithely regardless, alive, American, and unknowing amidst the miasma of history, "strolling along the top of one of those great mounds of ruin that are embanked with mossy marble and paved with monumental inscriptions" (43–4), Daisy comprehends her life principle lightly and perfectly: "If I didn't walk I should expire" (33), she tells an inaptly named Mrs. Walker. Mrs. Walker, representative of a society of parlors, never does walk, but chases Daisy in her carriage to persuade her against walking. "If I didn't walk I should expire," says the girl of gardens and the vibrant moment, surprised into opposition; and when she

65

cannot walk any longer, she dies, a latest Roman sacrifice to a world of rooms and rules.

These too are simple, her perfect understanding and her nasty doom. Daisy begins simply, fills out only to defend that simplicity, and expires into mythy apotheosis: the "most innocent" of all young ladies by the account of the cured opportunist Giovanelli (49), whose judgment is unimpeachable in an assessment that holds no stakes for him. James, amazed that readers followed Winterbourne in making Daisy's innocence a point of dispute, ever after seconded the Italian's judgment.[2]

Daisy's continuing and finally ennobled simplicity is not what we usually expect from fiction, where characters generally complicate themselves in the course of their experiences. But James means for us to see Daisy's complexity as not inherent. The terrible ambiguity, the vexing mystery of her status as innocent or vixen, have nothing to do with her inherent quality, simple as a Daisy can be; they are all evoked by Winterbourne's misshapen assessment. It is not really her story but Winterbourne's, and there the complications are killing.

Frederick Winterbourne does not go on or go too far, as he too accuses Daisy of doing. After his first words with Daisy, "He wondered whether he had gone too far; but he decided that he must advance farther, rather than retreat" (6). But his advances *are* half-retreats, and he vacillates throughout: hesitating to visit Daisy on his arrival at Rome once he hears of her as "surrounded by half-a-dozen wonderful moustaches" (25) or running comic opera between Mrs. Walker's carriage of imperial respectability and the scandalously free-walking Daisy. Progressively in the second, Roman half of the tale, Giovanelli succeeds Winterbourne as active suitor, and Winterbourne, retreating or receding, supplants the protective courtier Eugenio as eugenic guardian. Finally, spying Daisy with Giovanelli at night in the Colosseum, "as he was going to advance again, he checked himself; not from the fear that he was doing her injustice, but from a sense of the danger of appearing unbecomingly exhilarated by this sudden revulsion from cautious criticism. He turned away" (46), seeking secrecy for his hideous emotion, relief that now he can find surcease from his vacillating movements in the sure (but wrong) knowledge that Daisy is corrupt. Her goading causes him to turn again and advance, but only to scold Giovanelli, for Roman fever is potential in the dank night air of the ruins. This prudential warning is not so gallant, given that he had meant to retreat a last time before issuing any such warning, leaving Daisy to possible death – which he then goes on to cause, killing her spirit by his dismissal.

After Giovanelli's disclosure, Winterbourne confesses, "I have lived too long in foreign parts," the last and most shocking of many sexual puns in the tale. But then he goes round. "He went back to live at Geneva," where the contradictory rumors by which James's narrator introduces him are renewed, "a report that he is 'studying' hard – an intimation that he is much interested in a foreign lady" (50).

With Daisy, Winterbourne advances and retreats, recedes, and finally reverts. But without her he is motionless, he sits, he idles. That is how we find him in the garden of the hotel at Vevey, until Daisy's brother and then Daisy interrupt his stasis. In his very first description as "a young American," Winterbourne seems something other, a European idler; like one of Conrad's tropical emigrés, little is known about him. It is startling what we do not know about Winterbourne. Who are his parents? Has he siblings? We are told that he has many friends in Geneva, but only one male friend appears on the scene and that briefly, with information of Daisy at the Doria. Daisy is from Schenectady, her limitation but not her fault, but where is Winterbourne's hometown? Why, really, is he in Geneva, or in Europe at all? Where does he get the money to do nothing? What does he wish to do? He has been in bed with a woman, perhaps many, but has he ever loved? And what is he "studying" other than sex in Geneva and Daisy in this narrative?[3]

I think there are answers to some of these questions and answers to why we do not know the answers to others, awful disclosures about this "young American" who to Daisy "seemed more like a German" (7). The answers have to do with such matters as cash and class, labor and idling, sexuality and something that is its reduction and defeat. I am sorry the answers have to do with these subjects, so predictably present are such matters in the interpretation of books at our own cultural moment. But James knew his cultural moment, knew himself in it, too, and *Daisy Miller* is one of his many attempts to state the moment and to free himself from it.

I do not mean to deny the international theme that readers find in the tale but to sharpen it. James is certainly telling a story about cultural bigotry in which an American man who has neglected his origin has an opportunity to educate an American girl all too provincially limited, and by this interchange has an opportunity to go not "on" or "round" or "too far" but home. The necessary aging of young America is at issue. Daisy's death dramatizes a worry that the new nation cannot grow up into a world of vicissitude; and as all of Daisy's accusers are expatriate Americans, not one of them the real thing, James is warning, much as Mark Twain would do in limning the pretensions of the Mississippi River culture in *Huckleberry Finn*, of an American attempt to become culturally mature the wrong way, by grotesquely aping the nightmare aspects of European sophistication. When Mrs. Costello speaks of "the minutely hierarchical constitution" (13) of New York society, America appears feudal. In all this there is the sense of missed opportunity, not only for Daisy and Winterbourne, but for America and Europe to form that Jamesian compact in which American vitality and European knowledge and manners would combine to save the West. Yet there is something beyond the international theme, something that makes even Winterbourne's self-blame, put in the "lived too long in foreign parts" lexicon of that theme, half a misnomer and a rationalization, and I want to get at what it is.

2

Our questions about Winterbourne may resolve into a single, gigantic problem: What is it to be a man? In the American decades before the Civil War, a new definition of manhood was getting fashioned, and with a rapidity possible only in a new nation formed at a late stage of Western civilization. Industry, and the changes it effects in social organization and individual personalities, came pell-mell upon an America just learning to know itself. "Here, as in a theater," wrote James Russell Lowell, "the great problems of anthropology . . . are compressed, as it were, into the entertainment of a few hours."[4] An extremely insecure aristocracy, for instance, is barely established before it finds itself rudely jostled. "The older ideologies of genteel patriarchy and artisan independence were being challenged by a new middle-class ideology of competitive individualism," writes David Leverenz, adding, perhaps a bit too simply, "The new middle-class won, and its ideology of manhood as competitive individualism still pervades American life."[5] The significantly absent Mr. Miller is one such winner, remaining behind in what Winterbourne imagines his Italian rival would consider "that mysterious land of dollars" (41). But Winterbourne's confusion over Daisy suggests that commercially energetic America is a mystery to him as well, for Winterbourne is one of the losers in this redefinition of manhood. We know that he had been "put to school" (4) in Geneva by his parents at about the age of Daisy's brother Randolph. Familial wealth is the implication, supported as well by the circumstances and snobbery of Winterbourne's aunt. That is, Winterbourne comes from a shaky displaced aristocracy that has found a shaky home in Europe. In England, Leverenz notes, "a similar class conflict . . . had ended with the gentry re-establishing control by 1870,"[6] and although we might wish to complicate this assertion − labor certainly has some claims on an approved manhood in Victorian fiction − the defeat of the many socialist revolutions across Europe by forces of royalty in the 1840s did make the continent a more comfortable site for monied lassitude. America, Fenimore Cooper had written decades earlier, "possesses neither the population nor the endowments to maintain a large class of learned idlers,"[7] idlers such as Frederick Winterbourne, lifelong "student."

Thus Winterbourne's permanent vacation in Geneva is a choice; he has chosen not to enter into his own time and into the fray of "competitive individualism." This gives particular point to Daisy's characterization of Winterbourne's speeches as "formal" (20) and "quaint" (28). Winterbourne's lectures to Daisy on the nature of who is and is not a gentleman add to the anachronistic lexicon by which he seeks to assert his class superiority.

Winterbourne is willing to compete only by standards that rely on a code of behavior closely allied with inherited caste. He refuses free market competition and this refusal has everything to do with his romantic behavior. When Winterbourne abandons Mrs. Walker's carriage, apparently enlisting in Daisy's cause, he spies her with Giovanelli behind the same parasol prominent in his own first flirtation with her at Vevey, and the narrator's phrasing implies a major moment in Winterbourne's advance-retreat scenario: "This young man" (and the epithet focuses the issue of manhood) "lingered a moment, then he began to walk. He walked – not towards the couple with the parasol; towards the residence of his aunt, Mrs. Costello" (36) – where he can take his revenge in the sure condemnation of Daisy she will provide. He had done just the same on his arrival in Rome when he heard of Daisy surrounded by the moustaches; he will do the same differently when he hears of Daisy and Giovanelli in company again, retreating more aggressively to tell momma, informing Mrs. Miller that her daughter is "going too far" (43). When he does confront Daisy directly, it is as a parent, not a lover, lecturing her on propriety to the point that Daisy for once evinces resentment. She notes that Winterbourne has failed to offer her tea as a gentleman suitor should; and to his "I have offered you advice," Daisy rejoins, "I prefer weak tea!" (39), suggesting the degree to which Winterbourne dilutes his romantic presence by his learned condescension. In the Colosseum, when Winterbourne indicates to Daisy his condemnation, he does so by opting out of competition, telling her that "it makes very little difference whether you are engaged or not" (47). Daisy, echoing the phrase, soon says "I don't care . . . whether I have Roman fever or not" (48). In the tale's sentimental causality, Winterbourne's renunciation of interest in Daisy causes Daisy's renunciation of life. As he enters the Colosseum Winterbourne recalls Byron's description of it in *Manfred,* but he might better have recalled Manfred's confession that he killed his beloved, "Not with my hand but heart, which broke her heart, / It gazed on mine and wither'd" (II. ii. 118–19).[8] Winterbourne would rather kill than compete, and his response to challenge, tallying with the response of his class in arenas other than the romantic, is refusal and disdain.

"You needn't be afraid. I'm not afraid," Daisy tells him (16) when he is forced to admit that Mrs. Costello will not meet her, and we sense that Winterbourne fears more generally. Yet it is unanswerable whether he takes his aristocratic stance because he is afraid – of a world of change, of impulses in himself that would force him to choose against his lifelong choice of class – or whether he is afraid because he has chosen an aristocratic stance that demands the loss of what he calls "instinct" (10).

This is not to argue that James is, by contrast, glorifying the ascendancy of the mercantile class in America. As many readers have noted, the disorder of the Miller family, and forms of naiveté that approach the callow in Daisy herself, serve James as a harsh critique upon this class. Mr. Miller's absence from the family journey suggests a gendered distinction good for no one, as the man remains home making more money while the wife and children "get culture" (though never getting it at all). The son, Randolph, is "hard" as the lumps of sugar he criticizes, charmless, uncontrollable, and oddly "aged" with a voice "not young" (4). Europe to Daisy is "perfectly sweet" (9), the Colosseum "so pretty" (47), all with a reductive condescension that is the sweet echo of Randolph's jingoist convictions that American candy and American men are "the best" (5). Their mother suffers from a bad liver that is the equivalent of Mrs. Costello's headaches, these figures of opposing classes both substituting a narcissism of the body as pain for healthful purpose. The Millers too display a familial entropy that is a low result of the democracy that has advanced them. Mrs. Miller "is always wearing my things," Daisy laughs (17) as her mother appears wrapped in Daisy's shawl, but it's a significantly unfunny inversion of roles. Daisy is as much an unofficial orphan as Winterbourne, and the absence of appreciation and authority in her own family may well draw her to the paternalistic, culturally authoritative, and quaint Winterbourne.

Winterbourne cannot meet the challenge, however, for he and his female advisors are part of a fragile, essentially nouveau, American aristocracy that is not real aristocracy at all any more than these expatriates are real Europeans. The problem is less class division and prejudice than it is class confusion and anxiety. Winterbourne and his ilk make hyperbolic any true European conventions in order to stake a nervous claim to beyond-Miller status. "Real" Europe is problematic in itself as, in a commercial age, filthy lucre makes embarrassing appearances amidst the leisure of the European upper class. As early as the second sentence of the tale, the narrator notes of Vevey that "the entertainment of tourists is the business of the place" (3). The highest status hotel in Vevey, where the Millers reside, was built on the site of an old castle, both a reason for its status and a sign of the capitalist transformation of society. An actual establishment, its name, the "Trois Couronnes," implies both nobility and coins. The mishmash of the commercial and the aristocratic in Europe is one reason why its poetry-inspiring history is portrayed in the tale as dead-in-life, miasmic, not so much informing the present as sickening it.

Winterbourne too is financial, however much he wishes to disdain the world of economic struggle. As Ian Kennedy points out, when the narrator tells us that Winterbourne "had imbibed at Geneva the idea that one must always be attentive to one's aunt" just after he has described Mrs. Costello as "a widow with a fortune" (13), James uncovers the savage, selfish underpinning of the Genevan ideal of duty and of Winterbourne's fidelity to it and to his aunt.[9] In a sense, attendance upon his wealthy aunt is Winterbourne's job.

He has yet another, and Daisy points to it when, at Chillon, she senses that Winterbourne is returning to Geneva because of a liaison. Bravely turning her hurt to a sally, she taunts, " 'Does she never allow you more than three days at a time? . . . Doesn't she give you a vacation in summer? There's no one so hard worked but they can get leave to go off somewhere at this season, I suppose' " (24). No champion of freedom like Byron's Bonnivard, this prisoner of Chillon yet shares that hero's terrible adjustment to the loss of liberty.[10]

Even this momentary intimation of Winterbourne as prostituted makes his contempt for Giovanelli broadly hypocritical. On meeting the Italian, Winterbourne decides that "he is only a clever imitation" of a gentleman and he makes this claim in terms of labor: "He is a music-master, or a penny-a-liner, or a third-rate artist" (31–2). Winterbourne himself is, by occupation, no more and something less; and if Giovanelli indeed has "practiced the idiom" of speaking in English "upon a great many American heiresses" (31), one expects that Winterbourne has had to adapt to a few adopted idioms himself: "He had known, here in Europe, two or three women – persons older than Miss Daisy Miller, and provided, for respectability's sake, with husbands – who were great coquettes – dangerous, terrible women, with whom one's relations were liable to take a serious turn" (10). Who is the imitation of a gentleman? Giovanelli, by the unemployed Winterbourne's account, turns out to be a "perfectly respectable little man" who is in fact a *cavaliere avvocato* (41), and this gentleman lawyer ends by entering a plea for a true perception of Daisy's innocence. Just as the Italian takes Winterbourne's resigned place as amoroso in the narrative, though never in Daisy's affections, so too he takes Winterbourne's place finally in the reader's regard. Giovanelli is not Winterbourne's gigolo opposite so much as his double, and finally his better.

This then is the economic Winterbourne: an emigrant out of fear of practicing the American ideal of equal competition, an unemployed idler whose sense of aristocratic breeding is prostituted by fortune hunting. We must recall that Winterbourne is no confirmed villain, at least not until the final words of the tale when he refuses the true illumination, the grace of understanding his own character that Daisy's death has afforded him. His very attraction to Daisy is proof of a residue of possibility in him and of a desire for a non-Genevan self-reformation.[11] But the forms this attraction takes have everything to do with the class alliances Winterbourne had made; and when we ask, given such choices, what kind of manhood emerges, the answers constitute an encyclopedia of misogyny.

3

One of Henry James's great surprises is his occasional penchant for broad effects. I began by insisting that his basic plots are often melodramatic, and his naming of such characters as Daisy and Winterbourne is obviously allegorical. Noting such effects often makes James's reader queasy, and this is most true as regards the sexual puns. Can the Master, the writer's writer who provides the "sense of the sense," actually be thought to indulge in such adolescent double entendre? The answer is affirmative, for James will exploit the whole register of meaning making. The character always intends the more or differently figurative meaning of such words, the socially sophisticated meaning; but James intends all meanings, including those that betray the character's unsublimated self.[12]

The words that attach to yet another of Winterbourne's alter egos, Daisy's brother Randolph, offer such a case. Unsettlingly older than his age, Randolph's voice is "sharp, hard," his eyes "penetrating." He carries a long alpenstock, "the sharp point of which he thrust into everything that he approached –" (4). He "poked his alpenstock, lance-fashion, into Winterbourne's bench," calls the sugar Winterbourne has afforded him "har-r-d," and then "got astride of" the alpenstock (5). He speaks again in "his little hard voice," and converts his alpenstock finally "into a vaulting pole" (6).

Daisy's "small, slippery brother" (8) at times seems something of a walking penis; his aggressive energy – remeeting him in Rome, Winterbourne compares him to "the infant Hannibal" (27) – represents everything in American competitive manhood that Winterbourne had fled. Yet Winterbourne is not so apart from these tendencies and this phallicism as we first think.

Shortly after Winterbourne "wondered if he himself had been like this in his infancy, for he had been brought to Europe at about this age" (5), Daisy appears, and Winterbourne is described as "straightening himself in his seat, as if he were preparing to rise" (6). Much later, in Rome, Daisy on four occasions criticizes Winterbourne as "stiff." The social meaning of the adjective seems to oppose the romantic, as when Winterbourne tells Daisy he does not dance and Daisy replies, "Of course you don't dance; you're too stiff" (37). But I want to argue that the phallic condition of "stiff" opposes romance as well. The dance of respectful courtship demands flexibility and motion; the sexual love of women and men requires an appreciation of the entire person, not a stiff, phallic reduction of the Other. Daisy is right beyond her knowing when she refuses Winterbourne's request to "flirt only with me" because, in her words, "You're too stiff" (38). Just as Winterbourne attempts to live apart from his commercial age and thus becomes almost a fortune hunter, so in fleeing American competitive manhood and his own American "instinct" as he calls it, Winterbourne reduces his sexuality to the state of Randolph's, preadolescent and yet ever so hard.

James labors to establish Winterbourne's trouble at the outset, in Winterbourne's first meeting with Daisy, as he dramatizes Winterbourne's leaking libido in terms of an extended act of perception. This is how Winterbourne views the girl:

> They were wonderfully pretty eyes; and, indeed, Winterbourne had not seen for a long time anything prettier than his fair country-woman's various features – her complexion, her nose, her ears, her teeth. He had a great relish for feminine beauty; he was addicted to observing and analysing it; and as regards this young lady's face he made several observations.
>
> It was not at all insipid, but it was not exactly expressive; and though it was eminently delicate Winterbourne mentally accused it – very forgivingly – of a want of finish. (7)

In three sentences, James packs seven overlapping kinds of inhumanity, seven deadening sins. The first I would term *exploitative or acquisitive perception.* Winterbourne itemizes Daisy's features in such a way – her eyes, her teeth – as to make her an object or himself a horse trader. His "relish for feminine beauty" is resentable too. It suggests a practice of *connoisseurship,* an emotional distancing both affectedly aristocratic and somehow prurient, pornographic.

Seeing through the eyes of others is yet a third form of Winterbourne's blindness. Does the face lack a finish?, Winterbourne worries, and we worry that someone else is setting the standards. Note as we approach the passage that Daisy's glance is "perfectly direct and unshrinking" yet not "what would have been called an immodest glance" (7). Discrimination is a Jamesian essential, and naming is as natural as Adam, but this is the world's postlapsarian naming – "what would have been called" – not Adam's.

Winterbourne's *obsessive categorizing,* his classificatory zeal, is another function of his hand-me-down mentality. Earlier, when Daisy first appears, "she" is immediately made a "they" by Winterbourne: "How pretty they are" (6); and later, he questions, "were they all like that, the pretty girls who had a good deal of gentlemen's society? Or was she also a designing, an unscrupulous young person?" (10). Winterbourne will not allow women to be, will not grant them an integrating wholeness, will instead dissect and categorize. And when they don't fit, when humanity refuses such reduction – agreeing to Winterbourne's accusation, Daisy responds, "I'm a fearful, frightful flirt! Did you ever hear of a nice girl that was not?" (38) – he will dismiss them brutally, as he does at the Colosseum. Under an ominously "waning moon" (45), Daisy is revealed to him, all falsely, as unscrupulous indeed and he experiences his unbecoming exhilaration "by a sudden revulsion from cautious criticism." The cautious criticism is dehumanizing in itself, the bipolarities deadening. James has his final joke on Winterbourne when, after implying the gross inadequacies of the either-ors, he allows Daisy an innocence even in Winterbourne's dichotomizing terms. Winterbourne's "cautious criticism" of categories and types is his attempt to halt experience in aristocratic, hierarchical stillness; his final revulsion from it, itself fearful in a refusal to live with mystery, is less a refutation than an extension of it.

This categorizing has yet another aspect that constitutes his fifth sin of perception, one that we might call *testing*. In the early description of Daisy, Winterbourne tests her against various ideals of socially respectable appearances; and soon, in a moonlit scene that anticipates the finale in the Colosseum, Winterbourne suggests a boat ride to Chillon, primarily to see how far Daisy will go. Acceptance of the invitation would doom Daisy in Winterbourne's opinion and rid him of the bothersome ambiguities of his own creation, but for this pathetic relief he must wait upon Rome.

A sixth form of inadequacy in the early passage coexists with all the others, together constituting *the sins of the spectatorial*. As John H. Randall III writes, Winterbourne "sees life through the spectacles of the picturesque. What he responds to is a guidebook view of life, not life itself."[13] This marks him a cultural parvenu in his comments on the sights of Europe. When, for instance, he quotes Byron on entering the Colosseum, he reminds us of all those nineteenth-century American anglophiles who are described nicely by Benjamin Goluboff as "the alluder on the landscape," insecure travelers from the raw New World taking "a sort of examination in cultural literacy."[14] Winterbourne flunks the more crucial exam of understanding, for he is about to exemplify the final lines of Byron's Colisseum description, "The dead but sceptered sovereigns who will rule / Our spirits from their urns" (III. iv. 40–41).[15] Just so, when Mrs. Costello requests that her nephew bring her *Paule Méré*, she seems unaware that the Cherbuliez novel, published in Geneva, concerns the victimization of a brave woman, an older Daisy, by a weak husband reminiscent of Winterbourne and by a society much like Mrs. Costello's own.[16]

When Winterbourne directs this same effete, meaning-emptying appreciation toward Daisy, it bespeaks that removal from life that is also a removal from self. This self-removal provides another reason for Winterbourne's wish to visit Chillon with Daisy: "[H]e had never yet enjoyed the sensation of guiding through the summer starlight a skiff freighted with a fresh and beautiful girl" (19– 20). The sophisticated but crude "freighted" underlines once more the dehumanizing of Daisy, the "fresh and beautiful girl" the categorizing tendency of this collector of experiences. But there is also here a sense of Winterbourne, if you will allow me an anachronism, watching a motion picture of his own life. He can produce such a movie even when he is not present in a particular scene, as when he arrives in Rome and is discountenanced by the news that Daisy is surrounded by moustaches, "a state of affairs so little in harmony with an image that had lately flitted in and out of his own meditations; the image of a very pretty girl looking out of an old Roman window and asking herself urgently when Mr. Winterbourne would arrive" (25). This is uproariously self-flattering – Winterbourne Studios is consistently partial to its owner-star – but it is also self-negating, for one cannot live a life while obsessively observing it. Such self-consciousness even harms those attempts at manipulation that always undercut Winterbourne's moments of empathy. When he senses that Daisy is hurt by his aunt's refusal to meet her, Winterbourne decides it might be "becoming in him to attempt to reassure her. He had a pleasant sense that she would be very approachable for consolation" (16– 17). Winterbourne imagines unstiffening – though only in a most becoming way and only to get what his stiff self desires – but by the time Winterbourne Studios has produced the scene in his head,

Daisy's mother appears and his bad chance is lost. Life *is* for Daisy; it is always about to be for the screening room hero, though perhaps this is fortunate given his designs on it.

But Winterbourne is not a public actor, and if he creates his own scenes, he does not wish upon himself the eyes of others. He is secretive, and *guilty privacy* is his seventh sin. In the passage in which he itemizes Daisy's features, he is looking but his thoughts are not seen. This privacy is apt in a man who lives his only vital life behind closed doors and at absolute odds with the social manners he espouses so recklessly. James takes an early revenge on this hypocrite gossip by having his narrator speak of him in the falsely respectful, secretly savage voice of the society to which Winterbourne belongs:

> [W]hen his friends spoke of him, they usually said that he was at Geneva, "studying." When his enemies spoke of him they said – but, after all, he had no enemies; he was an extremely amiable fellow, and universally liked. What I should say is, simply, that when certain persons spoke of him they affirmed that the reason of his spending so much time at Geneva was that he was extremely devoted to a lady who lived there – a foreign lady – a person older than himself. Very few Americans – indeed I think none – had ever seen this lady, about whom there were some singular stories. But Winterbourne had an old attachment for the little metropolis of Calvinism; he had been put to school there as a boy. (4)

Each of the narrator's false hesitations to disclose something unpleasant constitutes a cut. The unseen lady – foreign, then older, finally singular in the stories told of her – is also Winterbourne's unseen life and suggests a reason for Winterbourne's interest in "coming off" with Daisy to Chillon secretly. He can thus deny her freshness and the jolt it might give to his pornographic, musty self. Winterbourne associates the libido with the hidden – that is why he despises meeting Daisy in the hotel hall (not simply because it is vaguely vulgar) and it is why, once they arrive at Chillon, he bribes the custodian to leave them alone, yet another act that characterizes his economic cheating. It is also why he cannot believe in Daisy's appearance of innocence, because his own appearance is so unnaturally fashioned to disguise what resides in Geneva and in himself. What Winterbourne half wishes is to make

Daisy taboo, for then she can enter his dirty little world and he will not have to leave it. That he also half wishes to leave it is what saves him a measure of sympathy. That he decides against this second chance is what ends all sympathy and dooms his manhood, as I will suggest a bit later, to a fate literally worse than Daisy's death because it constitutes damnation.

4

There is one element of Winterbourne's first long description of Daisy's appearance and of his entire encounter with her that is so obvious as to be hidden. It is best expressed in a law Leverenz constructs for Hawthorne's short story, "The Minister's Black Veil": "My wish to invade his privacy is an evasion of my own."[17] Winterbourne's invasion of Daisy's privacy, his dressed-up, vulgar desire to know, as Cathy Davidson puts it, " 'Does she or doesn't she?',"[18] is a way to evade questions about his own capacity for love. Troubled, frightened, Winterbourne runs from the world of male competition and surrounds himself with two kinds of women: the adultresses in Geneva and the prudish widows in Vevey and Rome. These two kinds are really one kind, halves of a determined double standard whereby, in Mrs. Costello's words, "a man may know everyone" (25).

Our major reaction is to exclaim against the women's society that castigates Daisy for wholly inoffensive and open actions while allowing for Winterbourne's hidden profligacies, "not morality but conformity," as William E. Grant writes.[19] And certainly we feel the force of female self-punishment: "[W]omen characters uphold the system which restricts them," Louise K. Barnett notes; and Davidson rightly calls these women "misogynous," adding that women like Mrs. Costello and Mrs. Walker "will seek to be men" and take on their authority.[20] But my main interest is in the degree to which Winterbourne submits to them. He "acquiesces in their power," writes Susan Koprince. He is, in Motley Deakin's summation, "the captive of women."[21]

He is the captive of both kinds of women. That he experiences the adultresses in Geneva as "dangerous, terrible" suggests a fearful subordination, suggested as well by Daisy's taunt that his present lover in Geneva will not even give him, her employee or servant, more than a few days off. Winterbourne thus does not appear sexually potent even in the gossip of his liaison with this woman about whom singular stories have been told. However wild the unnamed woman may be, he is emasculated by the relationship. Just so, when Winterbourne runs to Mrs. Costello or Mrs. Walker to discuss Daisy, curl his moustache as he may, he seems a woman himself. With Daisy alone, he becomes traditional male lawgiver; but Daisy, the one relief in this chaotic environment of misgendering, refuses him this authority: "I have never allowed a gentleman to dictate to me, or to interfere with anything I do" (31).

Winterbourne is castrated once more, but by Daisy less than by himself. He has taken this parental stance toward her, as I argued earlier, to avoid real competition. Indeed, Daisy's whole attempt with Winterbourne is to help him locate his manhood. This is the motive for all her teasing and taunting, to persuade him to behave as a man toward her but via love rather than authority. Thus when she is buried doubly inaptly – a Daisy dying in the spring, buried in cultural loneliness in the small Protestant cemetery in the world capital of Catholicism – James has his narrator describe her grave as a "raw protuberance among the April daisies" (49). Davidson sees here an Easter resurrection, with Daisy becoming "the patron saint of a repressed sexuality."[22] But Daisy's fate is Christlike only twistedly. When James earlier recalls the Resurrection by employing the phrase "On the evening of the third day" (36), he is referring to Mrs. Walker's party, where Mrs. Walker's snub makes Daisy look "with a pale, grave face at the circle near the door" (39). And the "raw protuberance" of Daisy's grave suggests a swelling in two ways ironic. As a female swelling, it is an image of death in the place of pregnancy, new birth, all that Daisy's youth and vitality promised. As a phallic protuberance, it suggests death's cause and Winterbourne's stiff loss.

Indeed, Winterbourne has entered forever the deadening, emasculating creed of what we might call the women's religion in *Daisy Miller*. I mean religion almost and terribly literally, for the expatriates' hellish code has usurped the place of the church. There is in fact a scene in St. Peter's where

A dozen of the American colonists in Rome came to talk with Mrs. Costello, who sat on a little portable stool at the base of one of the great pilasters. The vesper-service was going forward in splendid chants and organ-tones in the adjacent choir, and meanwhile, between Mrs. Costello and her friends, there was a great deal said about poor little Miss Miller's going really "too far". (42)

In this ugly scene, the women have taken to themselves the heavenly judgment that is St. Peter's office. And in the same paragraph Winterbourne hears from his friend of Daisy and Giovanelli viewing the portrait of Pope Innocent, a portrait the misnamed Pope himself called *troppo vero*,[23] as the renowned Velazquez painting reveals a cynic of worldly intrigue. The Pope's name underscores Daisy's own innocence while his face in the portrait, as Adeline Tintner writes, makes for "a vivid contrast" between the worldly head of state and "the secular, free-wheeling, free-thinking American Protestant girl who doesn't hesitate to turn her back on his Holiness and his so-called 'shrine.' "[24]

James gives us something of an encapsulated history of Western religion in this slight tale of Geneva, "the little metropolis of Calvinism" (4), and "the cynical streets of Rome" (42). With its accusatory conviction of innate depravity and its ability to live down to it, Geneva begins a process of destroying Daisy that Rome, city of ordained convention and the pernicious leavings of pagan and Christian history, completes. The attitudes of the expatriates who paganize the Church are yet the direct result of a long misprizing of the religious spirit by religion itself.

Entering the Colosseum, Winterbourne spies Daisy seated in the shadow of "the great cross in the centre" and, in Daisy's light words, he "looks at us as one of the old lions or tigers may have looked at the Christian martyrs" (46). But this is only the culmination of a process in which the expatriates translate religious and moral idealism into Victorian aggression devoid of real principle. Winterbourne finally adopts his aunt's view that "one does one's duty by not − not accepting" such Americans as the Millers (13). For Mrs. Costello, deep ethics is pretension: "Whether or no being hopelessly vulgar is being 'bad' is a question I leave to the metaphysicians" (25). Mrs. Walker, who wishes to convention-

81

alize Daisy rather than exclude her, does make metaphysical the socially conventional: She theologizes "Thank heaven I have found you," and, with "her hands devoutly clasped," attempts to persuade Daisy against walking in the company of men. "Extremely devoted" by the account of "certain persons" to the lady in Geneva (4), "awfully devoted" to Daisy in Daisy's joking phrase (20), Winterbourne finally takes his vows in the priesthood of the expatriates. Again, it is worth emphasizing that this is a choice, for Daisy, no metaphysician herself, has come to represent an alternative. Refusing Mrs. Walker's invitation to join her in her victoria for some moral instruction, Daisy says, "I don't think I want to know what you mean. . . . I don't think I should like it" (34); and the simple relativism of her "People have different ideas!" (38) gains a resonance against this creed of absolutism born of ennui and worse, a creed well defined by the narrator when he characterizes Winterbourne's thought of consoling Daisy as "a perilous mixture of gallantry and impiety" (17). But this emptying of the spirit succeeds in the world, leaving Daisy's memory and Henry James alone in opposition.

5

That is where Winterbourne ends, and in a moment we will name the place, but where does he originate? We do know Winterbourne's place in a literary sense, for this man of categories himself belongs to a category of male characters who populate nineteenth-century literature in America and England. He is the bachelor figure, bespeaking in the nineteenth century an anxiety of cultural exhaustion, the worry of a discontented civilization whose complaint is voiced by Winterbourne when he cannot type Daisy because "he had lost his instinct in this matter, and his reason could not help him" (10). The loss is not simply of the American instinct but of instinct itself – spontaneity, real awe rather than artificial appreciation, vitality, everything Daisy has and he lacks. Emily Brontë's Lockwood, George Eliot's Casaubon, Melville's gourmands in his "Paradise of Bachelors" who substitute the gustatory for the romantic and heroic, any number of Hawthorne's males who victimize women to their own destruction –

all are Winterbourne's literary kin. The bachelor, as I have written elsewhere,

> is a grotesque with an oversized intellect, a shrunken body, and a shrivelled heart. He refuses the human community; he will not risk relatedness, preferring to experiment on others or to observe them from a voyeuristic distance. Crippled by self-consciousness, if he loves he often runs away to maintain an equilibrium that is passion's defeat. Impotent and vengeful, highly intellectual but unwise, he sells his soul for a sullen invulnerability that is itself fraudulent, for his great need is to impress others.[25]

This is Winterbourne's literary lineage.

The bachelor is a function not only of over-civilization but of a tradition in male authorship in the Romantic period by which the femme fatale is cleared of charges. Such writers as Keats and Hawthorne engage misogynist legends that blame evil on women and rewrite them to redefine the evil as inherent in the manner that men view women; and this has everything to do with Daisy Miller and with James and *Daisy Miller*.

James's explicit allusions in the tale are to Cherbuliez and Byron, and the latter particularly has to do with that cultural fatigue we are describing. If Byron's heroes suffer an exhaustion of spirit from idealistic questing, Winterbourne, fleeing such quest while alluding to Byron, suffers *weltschmerz* squared and without glory, as a "Manfred Manqué," in Susan Koprince's phrase.[26] But the most powerful influences on *Daisy Miller* are not explicit. Central here is Hawthorne, about whom James was to write a full book in the next year. Richard Brodhead argues persuasively that "influence" is too mild a term to apply to the relation between Hawthorne and James, that James "perfectly internalized" Hawthorne from his earliest writings, giving fiction the dignity of internal literary history.[27]

Daisy Miller is such a thoroughly meditated variation on Hawthorne's tale "Rappaccini's Daughter" that it seems folly to enumerate the parallels – Winterbourne's resemblance to Hawthorne's Giovanni in their voyeurism, secrecy, failure of faith, and destructive conformity to an ethic of cynical skepticism parading as respectability; Daisy's resemblance to Hawthorne's Beatrice in their joint status as femmes fatales who are far more sinned against than sinning. It is more to the point to quote a single passage from Hawthorne: "Blessed are all simple emotions, be they dark or bright!" exclaims the narrator. "It is the lurid intermixture of the two that produces the illuminating blaze of the infernal regions."[28] In Winterbourne's case, while the "lurid intermixture" of his feelings prepares Daisy's doom, his demand for resolution seals it. In the "luminous dusk" of the Colosseum, with his "sudden illumination," Winterbourne unknowingly perceives via the darkness visible of his own sick spirit. Hawthorne's tale also connects James to Keats, for Hawthorne's Beatrice, poisonous yet pure, is herself a reminiscence of Lamia, the snake-turned-woman who captures a lover but sweetly, and who is destroyed by the lover's demand to show off his prize in a public wedding. She is ruined by his egotism and by his faith in a sophist teacher, Apollonius, the equivalent of Hawthorne's Baglioni and James's Mrs. Costello. Winterbourne stands with Giovanni (whose name, played upon, becomes Giovanelli and a better spirit in James's redaction) and Keats's callow, publicity-seeking Lycius as apparently pleasant if shallow youths who are yet male murderers.

But Hawthorne's tale goes back further, to an Italy older than Daisy's or Beatrice's. Beatrice was Dante's beloved, and the history of the poet's sublimation of his lust for her, to the point where he can experience God through her, is the ideal development that Hawthorne's Giovanni and James's Winterbourne fail miserably to achieve. Through Hawthorne, James reaches back to Dante's Rome – and to Dante's Satan, for Winterbourne's name is redolent of the Devil of the *Inferno*. Dante portrays a wintry Satan, devoid of all light and warmth, icily fixed in that loneliness that is the appropriate form of his utter self-love. The only motion available to Dante's Devil is the futile beating of his wings. Like Dante's lesser damned ones, like Winterbourne in the devastating final sentence of James's tale, Satan is condemned to endless repetition. The beating of his wings only fixes him more firmly in that ice which is the image of his hatred of others.[29] This failed motion, repetitive yet worsening, also characterizes Winterbourne, incapable of "going on" or "going too far," capable only of "going round" and getting nowhere, beating his wings. By this network of allusions, James is saying nothing so crude as that Satan is

Winterbourne's real identity. He is saying something worse, that this is the rough context for understanding what Winterbourne by his choices has made himself become.

But what has James become in the act of writing *Daisy Miller?* It is certainly possible that James was working through the premature death of his beloved iconoclastic cousin Minnie Temple, that Daisy is a less intellectual surrogate for this real woman who died at an early age.[30] For a more meaningful answer, we can refer to the relation between Hawthorne and another of his bachelors, Coverdale in *The Blithedale Romance*. As character-narrator, Coverdale bears a structural resemblance to Winterbourne, though James as narrator occasionally opens just enough narrative distance from his hero to satirize him, as in the early passage on what Winterbourne's theoretical enemies might say. Coverdale too is an idler, a more-and-more minor poet, a voyeur, an analyzer, a skeptic conformist, full of jealousy and lust and punished by the narrative into learning less and less of the truth of the individuals with whom he is obsessed. He misses all the major scenes, just as Winterbourne is progressively shut out of Daisy's life, staring at an occluding parasol. Yet in many ways Coverdale seems Hawthorne's avatar, for his refusal to share the utopian hopes of the Blithedalers mirrors Hawthorne's reaction to his summer at Brook Farm. So too, James, reaching a point in his expatriation where he might have feared "living too long in foreign parts," and, more important, opting out of that revolution in American manhood whereby the new middle class had established competitive individualism, a rivalry for dominance, as its leading principle, much resembles Winterbourne. What Irving Howe writes of Hawthorne and Coverdale may serve exactly for James and his Winterbourne. Howe notes the conflict in Hawthorne between a social self which "could summon no large enthusiasm" and "a powerful impulse within him" that "worked to assault and deride that scepticism." Thus Coverdale "is a self-portrait of Hawthorne, but a highly distorted and mocking self-portrait, as if Hawthorne were trying to isolate and thereby exorcise everything within him that impedes full participation in life."[31] This seems to me exactly true of James in relation to the materials we have discussed.

With one exception. I think James has achieved something better here and throughout his career than merely an exorcism. Leverenz notes that the writers of Hawthorne's generation sought a manhood that would refuse the old aristocratic requisites but also would avoid the new demands upon manhood of rivalrous individualism. Instead, he writes, they sought, by the creation of heuristic, unsettling narratives, to unseat themselves and their readers, to "fashion styles of self-dispossession."[32] Just so, James refuses the aristocracy of Winterbourne and the competing party of Randolph and Mr. Miller. That other alternative of self-dispossession, the one that feels what cannot be reasoned and questions all without the need for finality, is the manhood Winterbourne fails to locate and James practices. It is the site where manhood becomes ungendered and begins to become sexed humanity.

NOTES

1. Henry James, *Daisy Miller: A Study,* in *Tales of Henry James,* ed. Christof Wegelin (New York: Norton, 1984), pp. 6, 41. This text follows the first English edition published by Macmillan and Co. in February 1879. The work first appeared in the *Cornhill Magazine* of June and July 1878. Subsequent references are to the Norton edition and are cited parenthetically by page number in the text.

2. In his famous letter to Mrs. Lynn Linton, James wrote that Daisy "was, as I understand her, above all things innocent" and that "I did not mean to suggest that she was playing off Giovanelli against Winterbourne – for she was far too innocent even for that." See Leon Edel, ed., *Henry James Letters* (Cambridge: Harvard University Press, 1974 ff.), vol. 2, pp. 303–4. Yet critics often focused on Daisy's shortcomings, mistaking them for guilt, until and even at times after James W. Gargano first emphasized Winterbourne's centrality in *"Daisy Miller:* An Abortive Quest for Innocence," *South Atlantic Quarterly* 59 (1960), 114–20. Tamor Yacobi makes the most logically thorough case for Winterbourne as central in "Hero or Heroine? *Daisy Miller* and the Focus of Interest in Narrative," *Style* 19:1 (1985), 1–35.

3. James later said that he could not recall why he subtitled the first version of his tale *A Study,* but it may be that he wished to parody the cold examination of Daisy by Winterbourne, who is reportedly "studying hard."

4. James Russell Lowell, "Cambridge Thirty Years Ago," in *Works,* ed.

Charles E. Norton (Boston and New York: Houghton Mifflin, 1904), vol. 1, p. 16.

5. David Leverenz, *Manhood and the American Renaissance* (Ithaca and New York: Cornell University Press, 1989), p. 3.

6. Ibid., p. 4.

7. James Fenimore Cooper, *Notions of the Americans* (1825), excerpted in *The Norton Anthology of American Literature*, 3d ed., ed. Nina Baym et al. (New York: Norton, 1989), vol. 1, p. 852.

8. Lord Byron, *Poetical Works* (London: Oxford University Press, 1945).

9. Ian Kennedy, "Frederick Winterbourne: The Good Bad Boy in *Daisy Miller*," *Arizona Quarterly* 29:2 (1973), 142.

10. These points are argued variously by Carl Wood, "Frederick Winterbourne, James's Prisoner of Chillon," *Studies in the Novel* 9:1 (1977), 33–44; Carey H. Kirk, "*Daisy Miller:* The Reader's Choice," *Studies in Short Fiction* 17:3 (1980), 276; and Cathy Davidson, " 'Circumsexualocution' in Henry James's *Daisy Miller*," *Arizona Quarterly* 32 (1976), 365.

11. Nothing makes this clearer than James's dramatization of the tale. In it, Daisy and Winterbourne become engaged in the closing scene, one reason why *Daisy Miller: A Comedy in Three Acts* is a miserable failure.

12. This is not inevitable. In " 'Circumsexualocution' in Henry James's *Daisy Miller*," 353–6, Cathy Davidson nominates a number of such sexual puns which I find not wholly convincing. Mrs. Walker's admonition to Winterbourne to "cease your relations . . . to give her no further opportunity to expose herself" seems to me questionable. Nor can I agree that Mrs. Walker portrays a repressed lesbian desire for Daisy, much less that Daisy is guilty of "sexual exhibitionism" or an "insatiable appetite for male admirers" (pp. 361, 363, 364). This is not all wrong – Mrs. Walker's intensity does demand an explanation – but the accusation is.

13. John H. Randall III, "The Genteel Reader and *Daisy Miller*," *American Quarterly* 17 (1965), 575.

14. Benjamin Goluboff, " 'Latent Preparedness': Allusions in American Travel Literature on Britain," *American Studies* 31:1 (1990), 67, 66–7.

15. See Susan Koprince, "The Clue from *Manfred* in *Daisy Miller*," *Arizona Quarterly* 42:4 (1986) 299; and Randall, "The Genteel Reader," 577.

16. Motley Deakin classes Cherbuliez with Turgenev, George Sand, and Mme. de Staël as novelists in the European tradition whose independent, freedom-loving heroines influenced James's charac-

terization of Daisy Miller. See "Daisy Miller, Tradition, and the European Heroine," *Comparative Literature Studies* 6 (March 1969), 45–59.

17. Leverenz, *Manhood*, p. 230.

18. Davidson, " 'Circumsexualocution,' " 357.

19. William E. Grant, *"Daisy Miller:* A Study of a Study," *Studies in Short Fiction* 11 (1974), 22.

20. Louise K. Barnett, "Jamesian Feminism: Women in *Daisy Miller,"* *Studies in Short Fiction* 16 (1979), 281; and Davidson, " 'Circumsexualocution,' " 363.

21. Koprince, "The Clue from *Manfred,"* 300; and Motley Deakin, "Two Studies of *Daisy Miller,"* *Henry James Review* 5:1 (1983), 19.

22. Davidson, " 'Circumsexualocution,' " 356.

23. Jeffrey Meyers, "Velazquez and *Daisy Miller,"* *Studies in Short Fiction* 16 (1979), 173.

24. Adeline R. Tintner, "Two Innocents in Rome: Daisy Miller and Innocent the Tenth," *Essays in Literature* 6 (1979), 75.

25. Robert Weisbuch, *Atlantic Double-Cross: American Literature and British Influence in the Age of Emerson* (Chicago and London: University of Chicago Press, 1986), p. 120.

26. Koprince, "The Clue from *Manfred,"* 299.

27. Richard Brodhead, *The School of Hawthorne* (New York and Oxford: Oxford University Press, 1986), pp. 107 and 105–20 *passim.*

28. Nathaniel Hawthorne, "Rappaccini's Daughter," in *Tales,* ed. James McIntosh (New York and London: Norton, 1987), p. 195.

29. I am indebted to my colleague, Professor Ralph Williams of the University of Michigan, for his knowledge of Dante and for this summarizing characterization.

30. Alfred Habegger draws out the correspondences in two books, *Gender, Fantasy and Realism in American Literature* (New York: Columbia University Press, 1982) and *Henry James and the "Woman Business"* (Cambridge and New York: Cambridge University Press, 1989). In the latter, he examines Minnie Temple's letters, quoting her on "the absolute value of the individual" (p. 131), a more formal expression of Daisy's "People have different ideas," and he emphasizes both Minnie's "teasing directness" (p. 129), her impatience with affectation, and James's consistent defense of her iconoclasm against his family's disapprobation. Habegger attacks James for his comment on "the dramatic fitness . . . of her early death" and of "her future as a sadly insoluble problem." Habegger finds it inhumane for James to speak of how her "poor narrow life" could contain "no place for

her" (p. 144). In light of *Daisy Miller,* this seems to me not at all heartless.

31. Irving Howe, "Hawthorne: Pastoral and Politics," originally a chapter in *Politics and the Novel* (New York: Horizon, 1957); reprinted in the Norton edition of *The Blithedale Romance,* ed. Seymour Gross and Rosalie Murphy (New York: Norton, 1978), pp. 288, 290.
32. Leverenz, *Manhood,* p. 5.

Class, Sex, and the Victorian Governess: James's *The Turn of the Screw*

MILLICENT BELL

T HERE ARE many ways of looking for meaning in *The Turn of the Screw* – and there is the plausible view that such looking is itself deliberately teased and baffled by the author – but generally ignored is the possibility that it is about social classes and their relation to one another and about gender in this context. In fact, these interests, predominant in the history of the English novel, are powerfully present in James's story, intermingled or disguised though they may be with other elements. James's famous tale told by a winter fireside, when ghost stories are being matched for excruciation, has always reminded readers of an obvious gothic tradition; like the governess herself, we ask ourselves as we begin to read, "Was there a 'secret' at Bly – a mystery of Udolpho or an insane, an unmentionable relative kept in unsuspected confinement?"[1] What follows fulfills these expectations, providing gloomy atmosphere and unsolved secrets, and the ghostly presence, if not the hidden physical one, of a former female inhabitant of the old house where the governess has her adventure. But there is good reason also to set this story in the frame of another sort of fiction. It is a late instance of what, since the 1840s, had been called the "governess novel," which dealt with the peculiar social position of governesses in the upper or middle-class English household. The heroine of such a novel was a woman burdened with the task of upholding and transmitting the increasingly "Victorian" domestic ideal, though she herself was single and unable to count on the prospect of marriage; she was a "lady" in the nineteenth-century sense of the term, yet anomalously earning her own living.

The Victorian image of the governess was one James understood very well, though that image is unlikely to be visible to the modern

91

reader of his story.[2] It was bound up, first of all, with the development of the nineteenth-century lady of leisure. One remembers Mrs. Bennet's tart comment concerning Charlotte Lucas's departure for home: "I fancy she was wanted about mince-pies. For my part . . . *I* always keep servants who can do their own work; *my* daughters are brought up differently."[3] That a well-to-do woman had practically nothing useful to do even in her home was a visible demonstration of her father's or husband's affluence.[4] But the daughter of a gentleman who had lost his money could hardly fulfill this ideal; she had to help with the mince pies or work in someone else's home. In that other woman's household she relieved the mistress of a traditional task. The woman who employed a governess could delegate to her the maternal responsibility of inculcating in the young the morals and manners of her class as well as transmitting some accomplishments and knowledge. Thus, a girl who had once herself had a governess might retain something of a lady's status by assuming a part of her employer's role.

This exchange did not always work smoothly. In the 1830s and 1840s, there was much agitation over the situation of the "distressed gentlewoman" who had become a governess. The governess's hold on class membership and sense of familial relation in her employer's home was a fragile one. At any moment she might be dismissed, unlike an old housemaid or cook retained long past her usefulness. The indigent ex-governess's plight led to the formation of a Governesses' Mutual Assurance Society in 1829 and then to the Governesses' Benevolent Institution in 1841 with its aim to "raise the character of governesses as a class, and thus improve the tone of Female Education, to assist Governesses in making provision for their old age; and to assist in distress and age those Governesses whose exertions for their parents, or families have prevented such a provision."[5]

The girl of "good" family who became a governess was a demonstration of the vulnerability of the Victorian Lady to the effects of her father's mismanagement or profligacy or even to the more general effects of economic upsets in a male-managed world. Every middle-class woman, one contemporary writer noted, had either had a governess herself or knew some relative or friend forced to become one.[6] In the hard years following the Napoleonic wars bankruptcy often destroyed the security once provided for an unmarried middle-class daughter, and made her marriage without a dowry less likely just when women outnumbered men. She had no "respectable" hope of employment except teaching, at school or in the home, the children of more fortunate women of her own class, though in earlier decades women like herself had worked beside men at many trades.

In times of economic crisis like the "hungry forties," men of all classes were likely to be reluctant to see women become competitors for jobs outside the home, but they were not threatened by the sequestered governess. Confined to the home and doing a mother's task – though it was not her own home and she was not a mother – the governess only confirmed the idea that women should stay out of the general working world where men labored. Yet the potential threat of the salaried if underpaid governess was still felt. That she worked for pay at all was an issue. Not only did the fact that she was a lady and yet a worker for wages threaten the very definition of the lady – but the governess was a woman who might do other kinds of paying work if driven by necessity to do so, or even by choice, if she were allowed. Hence the absolute interdict against other kinds of work for the gentlewoman of slender means.

Yet, should the governess lose her place, what would become of her? She might slip disgracefully downward as a pauper or "worse." But her fall from gentility into the ranks of the working class seemed almost equal to the degradation of the "fallen woman." The definition of the feminine as embodied in the wife who gave herself freely both sexually and maternally was already threatened by the governess; that she took pay for maternal functions was ultimately as alarming to such an ideal as the prostitute's sale of wifely sexual services. On the other hand she might – though rarely, except in novels – ascend into the master class by marriage, thereby threatening the distinction between master and worker.

Probably because of such fears, as much as out of charitable concern, steps were taken to improve the governess's opportunities for training herself as a professional, strengthening her dignity and her claim on adequate compensation. One of the results, however, of this movement, conservative as well as charitable in its intent, was to initiate higher education for all women, and thus – ultimately – to bring more women into competition with men in other professions. Queen's College for Women was founded in 1848 with the design of improving the qualifications of governesses, yet before long many other women were drawn to take its courses. Elizabeth Rigby, Lady Eastlake, who wrote a much-quoted review of the 1847 report of the Governess's Benevolent Institution which included reviews of *Vanity Fair* and *Jane Eyre,* all published the same remarkable year, was a conservative commentator who disapproved of the founding of the college. She insisted that the governess's chief qualification was nothing more than her ladylikeness.

> Take a lady, in every meaning of the word, born and bred, and let her father pass through the gazette, and she wants nothing more to suit our highest *beau ideal* of a guide and instructress to our children. . . . The real and highest responsibility and recommendation of an English governess must ever rest more upon her moral than her literary qualification.

It was the essence of the governess's function that she preserve and perpetuate her own refinement – her mastery of academic subjects was less important.[7]

But, as this observer also noted, "the case of the governess is so much the harder than that of any other class . . . a being our equal in birth, manners, and education but our inferior in worldly wealth. . . . There is no other class which so cruelly requires its members to be in birth, mind and manners, above their station, in order to fit them for their station."[8]

A governess's sufferings were not merely economic. As I have said, she was likely to be an object of distrust to those who employed her. She had to be a lady to carry out her role but was surely not ladylike in working for her living and no social equal of leisured ladies. Paid at best no more than a housekeeper or butler, she was often also resented by the servants who worked beside her for holding herself above them. She suffered acutely from what the modern sociologist calls "status incongruity."[9] And her respectability and her obligation to uphold the purity of the nursery often meant celibacy; the world of courtship and marriage was closed to her. For those gentlemen whom she encountered within the household where she was employed, she was the "tabooed woman."[10] Yet she was often shut off from the rest of the world as well. Loneliness was the common complaint of governesses.

The idea of Edmund Wilson and others that the governess in *The Turn of the Screw* is the victim of hallucinatory delusions may be justified to some degree if we are willing to consider that she reflects a typology which had a basis in fact. It was often true that a governess was a depressed woman who might break down under the conditions of her narrow life. The Scottish physiologist Andrew Combe, in his widely read *The Principles of Physiology*, published in 1834, wrote, "The situation of governesses [is] one of misery and bad health, even where every kindness is meant to be shown to them...in many families, especially in the higher ranks, the governess lives so secluded that she is as much out of society as if she were placed in solitary confinement." The result, he thought, was "beyond question, that much unhappiness, and not unfrequently madness itself, are unintentionally caused by this cold and inconsiderate treatment."[11] It was said that, at this time, former governesses made up the largest number of female inmates in hospitals for the insane.[12]

Some of these tensions may account for the appearance of the governess, who had been only a secondary figure in earlier fiction, as the heroine of dozens of novels which sympathetically depicted her difficulties. Most of these are well forgotten as literature, and their topical interest is often reduced either to the formulae of "providential" fiction or to fashionable society romance in which the governess's problem was solved by her marriage to a nobleman. In Mrs. Sherwood's *Caroline Mordaunt* (1835), the heroine strives along the way of spiritual salvation, encountering dangers, until, like Bunyan's Pilgrim, she reaches religious illumination. The providential novel does not dispense with the English novel's traditional marriage close but it is generally by her marriage to a clergyman that its heroine realizes herself in a call to higher duty than human love. Lady Blessington's *The Governess* (1839), a "silver fork" novel about fashionable life, tells, on the other hand, the story of a bankrupt's orphan daughter who moves from one governess job to the next, suffering all the miseries of the governess's lot, until she is unexpectedly made wealthy by the death of a rich uncle and romantically marries a lord. Despite the differences between these two kinds of stories, the attributes of the governess heroine were remarkably consistent. Patricia Thomson, who has reviewed the genre of the governess novel, says

> she was bound to be a lady – preferably the daughter of a clergyman; she was always impoverished, unprotected, and, by virtue of her circumstances, reasonably intelligent and submissive.... In addition, because her tenure of what was usually a disagreeable post was involuntary, she was absolved from any suspicion of strong-mindedness in earning her living and thus was especially dear to the reactionary novelist.[13]

Whether pietistic or sentimental, the early governess novel had a clear social function. It was designed to show how the threats lurking in the condition of the distressed gentlewoman could be overcome by a good governess whose reward would be spiritual or worldly, as the case might be. The governess was celebrated as the conservator of class and caste rather than as a threat to the culture which had produced her and cast her into humiliation and insecurity. This literary stereotype persisted throughout the century despite the fact that governesses continued to be a special problem to the class that had bred them, intimately disquieting to well-to-do persons who might be indifferent to the sufferings of other working women.

James remembered what governesses had been in his American childhood in the forties and fifties; he understood the role of the Victorian governess as the guardian of middle- and upper-class values, a function still persistent in English families he came to know. He was also familiar with her type as represented in the governess novel (we are only beginning to realize how much he read of minor Victorian fiction).[14] At the start of the new century, horrified by the uncultivated tone of American female speech, he was thus reminded how governesses had once inculcated a ladylike voice along with other genteel traits:

> Such wonderments send one back, all yearningly, to those Early Victorian and Mid-Victorian governesses of English girlhood, daughters of country parsons and half-pay officers, heroines (while

their fashion lasted) of sleepy three-volume novels, whose meagre erudition, whose melancholy music, whose painting on velvet, it was so easy and so usual to deride, but whose deep-seated sense, whose cultivated and consecrated instinct, for the speech of the gentlewoman, the product of bowery rural homes uninvaded as yet by the strident newspaper, covered a multitude of sins. This lady's "use of the globes" may have been open to revision, but she was, in a thousand cases, an exquisite, an almost unconscious instrument of influence to a special end – to that of embodying, for her young companions, a precious ripe tradition. She often embodied it, doubtless, better than she knew – even though the most distinctly recognized of her functions was to conjure away, in the schoolroom, caught or communicated vulgarities. A fiercer age, at any rate, appears even in her own country to have pretty well done with her, if not with the tradition itself; perhaps indeed after extracting and assimilating all she had so sweetly and so dimly to give. More influences had wrought upon *her*, mere inspired, purblind transmitter, than she could have at all named, and it was precisely her price that she was the closed vessel of authority, closed against sloppy leakage, and that that is one of the ways in which authority can be conveyed. It is better to be reduced, under pressure of convenience, to that way than not to be able to recognize *any* way. How, meanwhile, over the vast American distances, is authority conveyed? We smile, on behalf of our sisters and daughters, at the lean, limited governess; we even smile at the good ladies of the higher French convents, with their so arranged and restricted scheme, but who were primarily responsible, during long years, for the basis of converse in the women of the "best society" the world was to know.[15]

The view of the governess as moral conservator – as well as the model of language and manners – plays a certain role, as will be seen, in *The Turn of the Screw;* it is the view of herself that James's Governess upholds. She sees herself as a "closed vessel of [*moral*] authority" – responsible not only for the "good breeding" but for the virtue of her pupils – in her opposition to the evil forces that have invaded Bly. We hear practically nothing about the academic lessons she offers Miles and Flora, who seem (especially Miles) to need little such instruction from her. It is illuminating to recall that in *What Maisie Knew,* published only a few months before *The Turn of the Screw,* Mrs. Wix, Maisie's "good" governess, is a specialist, above all, in "the moral sense." "Subjects" are quite scanted in Maisie's studies with either of her two instructresses, but this is not because she is neglected. As Lady Eastlake had said, it was the governess's moral qualifications that really mattered.

But James also saw the governess more complexly as a dangerous figure lurking somewhere in the Victorian consciousness along with this benign image and making for class instability. He understood the painful paradox of the governess's real position. The "lean, limited governess" was, he knew, often an unhappy woman or a neurotic one. As though in anticipation of the later story, that image was fleetingly evoked in "The Middle Years," published three years before *The Turn of the Screw*, in which a female companion to a wealthy dowager is said to have "a queer stare, naturally vitreous," which reminds one "of some figure . . . in a play or a novel, some sinister governess or tragic old maid."[16]

Though he remembered some novels depicting the less threatening type of governess in their "sleepy three volumes," James had a vivid awareness of two great and eccentric examples of the genre that recognized her unsettling possibilities. *Vanity Fair* deviates from the prototype of the governess whose final marital success is the reward of virtue; it presents, instead, a woman who sets out unscrupulously to capture a male member of the employer class. Thackeray's novel is picaresque as well as realistic, and though its keen view of all social levels is focused on the probable, the rise of its remarkable heroine was not a plausible prospect for the average English governess. Becky's rise reflected a persistent upper-class anxiety concerning the breaching of sexual and social barriers by the governess (or housemaid, for the tradition goes back to *Pamela*) who might be a temptation to her mistress's husband or son. Lady Eastlake liked *Vanity Fair*, probably for its warning picture.

Thackeray's novel is derisively parodistic of the governess novel. Its very title makes reference to *Pilgrim's Progress*, reminding the reader of how consciously the conventional governess novel of the providential type modeled itself on Bunyan's epic narrative. Becky Sharp is no Christiana. She never leaves Vanity Fair though one may say that she, too, is a lonely pilgrim bound for the Heavenly City; her Heavenly City is the ruling class. Thackeray also scorns the whole issue of the governess's situation as a distressed gentlewoman by making her a "sharp" young pretender who is simply the clever daughter of a bohemian artist and a French "opera girl." Her first adventure in upward mobility engages her with the Sedleys, themselves recently gentrified, and her brief spell of governessing for Sir Pitt Crawley's children by an ironmonger's daughter is an introduction to vulgarity in higher places. As a governess she has an appropriate indifference to formal study, but Thackeray gives this a sarcastic antimoral meaning: "With the young people, whose applause she thoroughly gained, her method was simple. She did not pester their young brains with too much learning, but on the contrary let them have their own way in regard to educating themselves, for what instruction is more effectual than self-instruction?"[17]

Becky Sharp produced some imitations in later Victorian fiction, like Wilkie Collins's Miss Gwilt, the amoral heroine of *Armadale* (1866), but James's only approach to a bad governess along Thackeray's lines is the secondary figure of Miss Overmore, Maisie's other governess. She, too, uses her position unscrupulously to climb into the security of her employer's class, marrying Maisie's father. And she is better credentialed than Becky; she is a genuine lady. As Maisie's mother concedes, she is "a lady and yet awfully poor. Rather nice people, but there are seven sisters at home." Maisie, comparing her to Moddle, the nursemaid who had previously looked after her, observes, "Miss Overmore never, like Moddle, had on an apron, and when she ate, she held her fork with her little finger curled out."[18]

But James is not greatly interested in the issue of class distinctions and their permeability in *What Maisie Knew*. That the second Mrs. Beale was a lady is as much a mockery of anything ever meant by the term, as in the case of Maisie's mother. *What Maisie Knew* uses as its only moral backboard the rather dowdy virtue of Mrs. Wix, whose other credentials as a governess are probably inferior to her glamorous rival's. The bad governess of the Thackeray type did not, in any case, take such hold on James's imagination as did the example to be found in the other great, unconventional governess novel – which Lady Eastlake didn't like – Charlotte Brontë's *Jane Eyre*.

In this highly personal masterpiece Brontë mingles the treatment of real social issues with romance and combines the governess genre with the gothic in the fire of a revolutionary imagination; she romantically rewards her intense, willful, sometimes neurotic heroine with marriage to the master only after Jane has tamed his arrogance. Unlike *Vanity Fair, Jane Eyre* gives a serious, if individual interpretation to the providential aspect of the governess novel. As Jerome Beaty has argued, Brontë's novel may be seen as "essentially the story of Jane's increasing awareness of the role of Providence in her life."[19] But a powerful wrench away from the model of *Caroline Mordaunt* enables Jane to reject the generically prescribed loveless marriage to a clergyman, St. John Rivers, and marry Rochester – for love (though even this romantic ending takes place in a twilight of muted passion). James's governess tale lacks either a providential or a sentimental conclusion, yet *Jane Eyre*, as I shall show, is the story his heroine herself dreams of having, the rejected plot against which her history strains. Despite the differences, James's story is powerfully haunted by the example of *Jane Eyre*, borrowing openly its gothic aspect, influenced more covertly by its themes of class and femalehood. And, as in *Jane Eyre*, the gothic element gives the realist themes symbolic form.

When James published *The Turn of the Screw* in 1898, the governess issue was no longer the conspicuous public question it had been earlier in the century. The "redundant" genteel spinsters who had been deplored by W. R. Greg in 1862[20] now found other respectable occupations – as schoolteachers, with the expansion of schooling for girls as well as boys; as nurses, after Florence Nightingale's demonstration of the need for that profession; and in the world of business and commerce, as clerks and secretaries. *The Turn of the Screw* was probably one of the first of James's works to be dictated "to the typewriter." His typist was a man, but women were seizing hold of this new occupation and three years later James replaced him with a woman. He told a friend, "he's too expensive. I can get a highly competent little woman for half."[21] Yet the issues of class raised by the governess earlier in the century were still fundamental in English society. James summons them into view by an apparent archaism, revives the example of *Jane Eyre*, and sets back his tale to the revolutionary decade of the forties.

The frame of *The Turn of the Screw*, often discussed as though it were only a device to increase the ambiguity of the story by qualifying the reader's sense of direct contact with the governess, gives us a sense of historical perspective. James's opening reproduces an actual country house visit when he had heard the "germ" of his tale; this present dissolves into the youth of Douglas when the governess told *him* her story and then into the more distant time of the story itself, when the events she described took place. Douglas's acquaintance with the governess – who has been dead twenty years – "was long ago and this episode was long before." He gives us his view of her – which may not be identical with that of the reader – and transmits her manuscript, written, of course, "in the most beautiful hand" (2). He clearly sees her as an ideal governess of earlier days, a lady with every appropriate sign of grace and breeding, though fallen on hard times. She is fit to be heroine of a providential governess novel in her dedication to the welfare of her charges.

She is also fit for that romantic reward that awaited the fictional governess who was loved by a gentleman. So "awfully clever and nice," she seems to have aroused the love, much later, of young Douglas, when she was his sister's governess. "She was the most agreeable woman I've ever known in her position; she'd have been worthy of any whatever" (2), he says. The anonymous narrator guesses, without clear foundation – though Douglas concedes that his story will confirm it – that at Bly "She was in love" (3). Like so many governess heroines – and like the Brontë sisters – she is the daughter "of a poor country parson" (4) who has left her economically straitened family to seek employment. When, in the middle of the story, she tells us she has received bad news from home we can imagine that this news concerns her family's economic difficulties. She is an innocent girl of twenty when she is interviewed in Harley Street by the nameless man James calls "the Master."

He, too, is a familiar type, "a gentleman, a bachelor in the prime of life," an inhabitant of the world of "high fashion, of expensive habits, of charming ways with women." He is out of the genre, too – "such a figure as had never arisen save in a dream or an old novel" (4) before the fluttered, anxious girl. He is, potentially, Rochester, whom Brontë could not help making attractive despite her constant insistence that he is not good-looking. That Rochester also inhabits the world of fashion and can be charming to women is shown in the chapters which describe the "merry days" at Thornfield when he entertains his society friends and flirts with Blanche Ingram. The gentleman in Harley Street represents what is now inaccessible to the governess – the glamor of affluent upper-class life.

There may also be something mysterious in his past, a latent Byronic darkness. Like Rochester, he seems to have no wife, but he has children on his hands – as Rochester has little Adèle – the burden of whose care he would place on the Governess. Brontë allows Adèle's origins to be somewhat doubtful though she asks us to accept Rochester's denial that this child of a former mistress is his child also. Something similar happens in *The Turn of the Screw*, particularly because we cannot help remembering its Brontë model, which hovers over James's story so insistently. We can be tempted to believe that Miles and Flora are the Master's own children.[22] We may even be inclined – though the fit of the hypothesis is poor – to wonder if they are not the children of Miss Jessel, the Governess's predecessor, as Rochester's mistress and wife are Jane Eyre's predecessors. The suggestion lingers despite the fact that we are expressly told that Miles and Flora are the children of a younger brother who died in India. Though we will probably curb these impulses to strike a parallel, generic expectations add something of Rochester to the Master's slightly indicated character and we suspect him of possessing qualities which make him dangerous to women. He is felt to embody masculine and class authority in its most privileged and insidious form whether or not he actually exercised "seignorial rights" over the dead governess. On the living Governess he has at least brought to bear all the force of his sexual magnetism and the power of his wealth; he has offered her a salary which "much exceeded her modest measure," and he has appealed to her womanly sympathy in his predicament. She is unable to refuse a situation "of serious duties and little company, of really great loneliness" (6).

Generic expectations are going to be frustrated in James's story although Douglas's friend, who has heard this much, is sure he knows the ending – "The moral of which was of course the seduction exercised by the splendid young man. She succumbed to it." "She saw him only twice," Douglas says, disappointing one of his lady listeners. He says that when the fine gentleman held the Governess's hand and thanked her for her sacrifice, she already felt rewarded. "Was that all her reward?" this listener, who has read too many governess novels, protests. And Douglas insists, letting the reader know in advance that more may not be expected, "She never saw him again" (6). It is clear that she never marries, though James's Governess has no full novelistic history; hardly more than a short story in length, *The Turn of the Screw* is only an episode in a life which continued. In this respect her history is more true to probability than most governess novels, including Thackeray's and Brontë's. The curious relation of James's heroine to the Master is founded on the reality of the governess condition which generally forbade reentry, by marriage, into the class of masters. The Victorian governess was expected to police the emergence of sexuality in the children in her charge and to be, herself, the "tabooed woman," and James makes his Governess more tabooed than any real governess by the absoluteness of her employer's prohibition of communication with him. James's Governess only fantasizes a romantic annulment of the taboo.

If governesses were notoriously lonely, absolute loneliness is what this governess suffers at Bly where *no* member of the children's family is ever to be met and no company comes. With the housekeeper, Mrs. Grose, her relationship is certainly almost affectionate and dependent; it resembles that of Jane Eyre and Mrs. Fairfax. But the Governess's vision, in the end, is one that an ordinary servant cannot share. Here, too, she must suffer isolation. Her own perceptions – or the other's common sense – separate them as does their difference of class origin. With that class from which she has been exiled there is no hope of a recovered relation.

But if the reader knows that the Governess will not reenact Jane Eyre's consummation, the Governess herself does not. She comes to Bly in a mood to see it as a "castle of romance" (10), or as another Thornfield over whose crenellated roof rooks circle as they had over Rochester's secluded house. She feels ready to figure in a romance. "Wasn't it just a story-book over which I had fallen a-doze and a-dream?" (10). From the first, Bly invites her to dream of a translation from the humility of her own "scant home." Mrs. Grose greets her "as if [she] had been the mistress or a distinguished visitor," the first of these "as if"'s anticipating a future as the Master's bride. She is moved by the liberality with which she is treated: "The large, impressive room, one of the best in the house, the great state bed, as I almost felt it, the figured full draperies, the long glasses in which for the first time, I could see myself from head to foot" (7) – that full-length view seeming to suggest a more liberal measure of selfhood than her past has provided. And to Mrs. Grose she admits, without being censured as Mrs. Fairfax censures Jane for falling in love with Rochester, that she has been "carried away in London" (9).

It is the Master of whom she is dreaming, hoping against all possibility to see him violate his own denial of romantic narrative, when she first sees Quint:

> It would be charming as a charming story suddenly to meet some one. Some one would appear there at the turn of a path and would stand before me and smile and approve. I didn't ask more than that – I only asked that he should *know;* and the only way to be sure he knew would be to see it, and the kind light of it, in his handsome face. (15)

The frustration of this expectation by the substitution of the valet's apparition is a repudiation of James's models, or, rather, a dark inversion of them. For Quint, one may say, *is* the Master. He is his double, dressed in his clothes and, accustomed to take the Master's privileges, "free" with those in his power, especially young women like the Governess and her predecessor. He is the Master in his aspect of callous seducer, the man who may have ruined Miss Jessel – who also had been a lady, as Mrs. Grose remembers. That the Governess can see the Master as Quint or that Quint is his double is an acknowledgment from somewhere in the Governess's own mind, perhaps, but certainly in James's, of the menace of the Master.

For though she has been "carried away" and continues to dream of pleasing him by her fidelity to his charge, the fact is that he has abandoned her – even if it is true that they only met twice and he could not have done more than smile and hold her hand. Her case is no different, potentially, than if he had "had his way" with her sexually. For is not this what has happened to *her* double? It seems obvious that the earlier governess had also been "carried away" in Harley Street. "Miss, you're not the first – and you won't be the last," Mrs. Grose tells the new Governess.

Douglas will say that Miss Jessel had been "a most respectable person" (5), and Mrs. Grose tells the present Governess that her predecessor "was also young and pretty – almost as young and almost as pretty, Miss, even as you" (12), and that she was "a lady" – establishing their similar qualifications as governess heroines. But one of Douglas's auditors is prompted to ask, "And what did the former governess die of? Of so much respectability?" (5). The ambiguity here is suggestive. On the one hand, a certain skepticism concerning that "respectability" is implied; on the other it is suggested that the *cause* of her death was her respectability.

We may speculate as to whether her own sense of virtue, her "respectability," was not destructive to Miss Jessel; we will find it a mortifying burden to our Governess. But if her respectability can only be referred to ironically we have to consider whether the cause of Miss Jessel's death, which cannot be named, was not simply a pregnancy following forbidden sexuality – her disgrace ending in death being a consequence and a punishment which did not need to be explained to the Victorian reader. Douglas promises that his story will answer his questioner. "That will come out"(5), he says. We have reason, therefore, to study the Governess's tale to find what Miss Jessel died of. We are not *told*, but does not our imagination take the short step to the thought that she died pregnant or in childbirth?

If so, what man was responsible? The readiest answer is Quint. The Governess suspects "there was something between them," and Mrs. Grose admits more: "There was everything"(33). Quint had been "much too free ... with everyone"(26) he "did what he wished ... with them all." When the Governess says that this "must have been also what *she* wished," Mrs. Grose does not deny it, but merely observes, "Poor woman – she paid for it!" – and we know, in our conventional minds, just how a woman "pays"! Mrs. Grose is nearly explicit when she says that as for what Miss Jessel died of, "I wanted not to know. I was glad enough I didn't, and I thanked heaven she was well out of that." But as to the real reason for her leaving, "she couldn't have stayed. Fancy it here – for a governess! And afterwards I imagined – and I still imagine. And what I imagine is dreadful"(33). "Fancy it here – for a governess!" What anomaly could have been more shocking than a pregnant governess? Has the displaced gentlewoman justified Victorian anxiety about her precarious ladyhood – anxiety which anticipated the transformation of this guardian of sexual propriety into the illustration of sin? In addition, her transgression of sexual limits has also been a transgression of social boundaries if she, a lady, has had an affair with Quint, who was no gentleman.

If it is pretty clear that, as Mrs. Grose believes, the dead governess was seduced by Quint, how can we argue for the guilt of the Master? For a declassed person, a hired governess whatever her original station, social barriers would have been violated even more by a sexual relation with her superior. We arrive again at an answer not evidentially true but true symbolically if we see Quint as a projection of the Master's potentiality. Quint *wasn't* a gentleman, but he appears in the *masquerade* of a gentleman – in his master's clothes – and he has assumed his master's prerogative to express the demonic side of maleness and class power in the Master. This hidden aspect of the Master the living Governess may suspect just as she suspects her own identity with the doomed Miss Jessel, her own susceptibility to Miss Jessel's fate.

The doubling that makes this evident is reinforced by another, that of the Master with little Miles. "Master" Miles, as he is called, homophonic coincidence aiding, is a miniature of the Master, dressed, if not in the Master's clothes, at least by the Master's tailor – the "little gentleman" by whom the Governess will be "carried away"(9), as Mrs. Grose predicts, as she had been by the uncle. He is beautiful as the most beautiful child can be, but his is a male beauty, irresistible to the Governess as the Master's handsomeness had been. But even before he arrives home, dismissed from his school, his glamor will be tainted by the letter which does not name his fault. Though the Governess speaks of it as probably the "corruption" of his schoolmates, the nature of the boy's offense is not made explicit any more than the probable corruption of the Master. James leaves it to the reader to fill in the "blanks"[23] from his own experience, and it may be, as Richard Ellmann has suggested, that for the Victorian reader that filling-in would be the imputation of homosexual behavior.[24] What is more important is the suggestion, deliberately vague, that Miles is a general source of sexual or other danger, even to the Governess herself. "Are you afraid he'll corrupt you?" Mrs. Grose challenges with a laugh – but the question is real. The Governess *is* afraid that she will be corrupted, this time by the Master as his tiny avatar, little Miles.

For she falls in love with the child, just as she has with his uncle. Sexual love between adult and child is a violation of taboo even more outrageous than love between the classes. To suspect Miss Jessel and Quint of molesting Flora and Miles – either homosexually or heterosexually – is to fill in another way, the blank of their undenoted evil by something well known in Victorian as in our own times; indeed, contemporary memoirs suggest that upper-and middle-class Victorian men were often "initiated" by servants, and even by governesses.[25] But the living Governess's feeling for Miles is also perhaps sexual, even if unconsciously so. It is at least an instance of a situation more common and generally quite innocent, that compensation for loneliness which the isolated governess, bereft of other objects of affection, might seek from the children in her charge. In the case of James's Governess, love for the child is not only an amelioration of her distance from his uncle, but a *representation* of her feeling for him. And Miles's responses to her no less represent, as in a dream, the Master as lover.

"I was under the spell . . . I gave myself up to it," she says, and never asks Miles to explain what happened in school; she would rather not know, just as a woman in love would rather not know the bad past of her lover. For her, as for other governesses, formal school lessons seem less important than other aspects of her relation to the children in her charge, but it was she who seems the student, and what she studies is a new hedonism rather than an old morality. She turns her back on her own severe upbringing and gives herself up to the delights of immediate experience as it comes:

> I learnt something – at first certainly – that had not been one of the teachings of my small smothered life; learnt to be amused, and even amusing, and not to think for the morrow. It was the first time, in a manner, that I had known space and air and freedom,

> all the music of summer and all the mystery of nature. And then
> there was consideration – and consideration was sweet. Oh it was
> a trap – not designed but deep – to my imagination, to my delicacy,
> perhaps to my vanity; to whatever in me was most excitable.(14)

She has succumbed to an attitude toward life she could have
learned from that charming man-of-the-world, the Master.

It was a trap, for the "spell," she suspects, may not be benign.
She does, after all, want to know the truth about her pupil's character, about who he is. She fears to find – but perhaps rightly
detects – a demonic self that coexists with Miles's angelic beauty
and perfect behavior. For the Governess, the parson's daughter,
there is nothing figurative about the word "demonic"; she is ready
to think of Miles not only as angelic but as quite literally possessed
by the red-haired Quint who reminds some readers of traditional
descriptions of the devil.[26] She suspects him of a concealed "intercourse" (37) with this satanic representative of his uncle.

I have said that she has reason to feel herself abandoned by the
man who will not allow her to continue the romantic governess
tale with him, and that her case is not separable from that of Miss
Jessel, who must have been betrayed and abandoned by someone.
But it is Miles who, in *his* role as the Master, makes this evident
on that Sunday morning when he demands, speaking so "charmingly," like a grown man, "Look here, my dear, when in the world,
please, am I going back to school?" She is not unaware of whom
she is dealing with.

> Turned out for Sunday by his uncle's tailor, who had had a free
> hand and a notion of pretty waistcoats and of his grand little air,
> Miles's whole title to independence, the rights of his sex and situ-
> ation, were so stamped upon him that if he had suddenly struck
> for freedom I should have had nothing to say. I was by the strangest
> of chances wondering how I should meet him when the revolution
> unmistakably occurred. I call it a revolution because I now see how,
> with the word he spoke, the curtain rose on the last act of my
> dreadful drama and the catastrophe was precipitated. (54–5)

His tone and the repetition of the "my dear," which, the Governess observes, "was constantly on his lips for me," continue in
a colloquy curiously adult. "You know, my dear, that for a fellow
to be with a lady *always* –" he begins. Her laughing, feminine

response plays with his words as though he were a lover growing bored, a man who wants a change of mistresses – "And always the same lady?" He catches her nuance perfectly, "Ah of course she's a jolly 'perfect' lady; but after all I'm a fellow, don't you see? who's – well, getting on." Why does his effort to break free seem a "catastrophe" to her, so that, she remembers, "Oh but I felt helpless" (55)? That he is stronger than she is evident when he threatens to write to his uncle.

Miles only wants to go back to school and be with other boys, but he puts it like a man who wants to move out of the confinement of a first love affair: "I want to see more life... I want my own sort" (56). What is his own sort? No longer boys, for he is "getting on," but men, a world from which the Governess, being a woman, is excluded. But also his own *social* sort, to which the upper-class lover is bound to return, leaving his governess mistress behind. She is a jolly "perfect" lady – the quotations about "perfect" remind us of the Governess's qualifications – and yet she is not for marrying.

Why is she so terrified? What if the Master does come down to clear up the mystery of Miles's banishment from school? Why should she panic, thinking that she must bolt and "put an end to [her] ordeal by getting away altogether," driving "desperately off" that very moment? Is it not because she realizes that she has tried – improperly – to hold the boy and that he will not be held? Returning to Bly with the idea of flight in her mind, she sinks at the foot of the staircase "with a revulsion, recalling that it was exactly where, more than a month before, in the darkness of night and just so bowed with evil things, I had seen the spectre of the most horrible of women" (58–9). For now she understands the meaning of Miss Jessel's despair and her own identity with this "vile predecessor"! Opening the schoolroom door she sees her double again, seated at her desk and writing with her pen and ink, like some housemaid, she thinks, who has stolen in to write a letter to her sweetheart. If Miss Jessel, "dishonoured and tragic," is writing such a letter, to whom is it addressed if not to the absent Master who has forbidden the living Governess to write him? It is at this moment that the Governess resolves to write the Master herself.

She does not leave. Instead, she stops outside Miles's bedroom that night and is gaily summoned in by the masterful little man, who tells her that she sounded "like a troop of cavalry" when she thought she was undetected. He has been lying awake thinking, and to her question replies, in loverlike and calculated tones, "What in the world, my dear, but *you?*... also, you know, of this queer business of ours... the way you bring me up. And all the rest." Why is it a queer business and what is "the rest"? "Oh you know, you know," he merely answers. Forced to treat him as "an intelligent equal," that is, an adult, she will insist, "I thought you wanted to go on as you are," and prompt from him a more urgent, "I don't − I don't. I want to get away." No, he's not tired of *Bly*, it's not Bly − "Oh *you* know what a boy wants" (62−3), he tells her.

Is not sex what a grown boy, what a *man* wants? It's not to go back to school. "I want a new field" (64). She deludedly thinks it is only pity for him, bound to suffer again for a repetition of past sins, that makes her throw herself upon him. She embraces him with "Dear little Miles, dear little Miles." He lets her kiss him, "simply taking it with indulgent good humour. 'Well, old lady?' " though his final word is that she is simply "to let [him] alone." But her desire to know him fully, to make him tell her "what happened before" makes her drop down beside his bed to "seize once more the chance of possessing him," her own "possession" supplanting that of Quint. The window shakes with a great wind, the child shrieks, the candle goes out. Is it Quint? Is it the force of passion? "It was I who blew it, dear!" (65), says Miles, as if he were a lover darkening the chamber of love.

After this the Governess has her traumatic encounter with Miss Jessel and little Flora at the lake which results in the child's frantic "Take me away from *her!*" (73). The climax has been reached in the realization of her inability to save from demonic influence the little girl who is a representative of herself. It is easy, in the face of the paramount importance of Miles in the story, to overlook the role James has given to his sister. Flora is the remnant, to begin with, of James's fidelity to the example of *Jane Eyre*, which offers only a single child, a female one, as Jane's responsibility at Thornfield. Originally, James's Governess was to be chiefly responsible for Flora and to have the care of Miles only during holidays; it is Miles's unexpected expulsion from school that puts her in charge of a male child of school age. By this deviation, James's plot, which involves most of all the Governess's obsession with the infractions committed by Miles at school as well as with his relationship with Quint at Bly, is initiated. A further "turn of the screw" is effected not only by the appearance of ghosts to two children instead of one, but by a doubling which produces miniature refractions of both the Governess and the Master.

Flora seems an exquisite blossom of perfect presexual innocence; she embodies the purity of the good governess. She completes the symmetry that poses her in contrast with Miss Jessel as Miles is posed in contrast with Quint on opposite sides of the Governess and the Master. Nevertheless, the Governess suspects the little girl of a corruption equal to Miles's. Her exchange of place either with the Governess or with Miss Jessel is made evident in such a moment as that in chapter 10 when the Governess finds Flora looking out into the garden from her bedroom window. Thinking to have caught the child in communion with Miss Jessel the Governess is herself challenged: "You naughty: where *have* you been?" (42). If, indeed, it is the Governess who is to be looked for in the dark night outside then it is, again, she who is identified with Miss Jessel while the watching, reproving child is the Governess. Immediately, the Governess sees from the head of the stairs the figure of Miss Jessel bowed "in an attitude of woe" at the bottom. What she says is also ambiguous in its suggestion of place-changing: "I had been there but an instant, however, when she vanished without looking round at me. I knew, for all that, exactly what dreadful face she had to show, and I wondered whether, if instead of being above I had been below, I should have had the same nerve for going up that I had lately shown Quint" (43).

She had already forced on Flora an identity with herself when she insisted that the child see what she sees, the specter of Miss Jessel across the "sea of Azof." In chapter 19 she again visits the lake to find that Flora has taken the boat across the pond, a feat beyond her childish strength — except that, as the Governess says, "at such times she's not a child: she's an old, old woman" (69) — as though she has already reached the age of the Governess and

Miss Jessel and gone beyond it to the ultimate adult distance from childhood's innocence. The Governess's accusation that Flora shares her perception of Miss Jessel brings upon her Mrs. Grose's reprobation, but, on the instant, in the Governess's vision, "her incomparable childish beauty had suddenly failed, had quite vanished . . . she was literally, she was hideously hard; she had turned common and almost ugly" (72–3). After this, even Mrs. Grose remarks that the experience "has made her, every inch of her, quite old" (74). Flora is, in a word, Miss Jessel, and potentially therefore the Governess herself, and later she will speak such "horrors" as only adult depravity could have done. More than depraved, moreover, Flora may be "ill" (81) as the Governess admits to Miles, that is, *mad*, with the madness that Victorians believed to be the punishment for depravity. She recalls Brontë's hidden madwoman, Bertha Rochester, who is said to speak more foully than a "professed harlot" – and reminds one of the hint of madness about even the Governess herself, who at least once, along with the reader, wonders if she is mad.

With the departure of Flora and Mrs. Grose, the Governess is left alone with Miles, to enact the terminus of their "queer business." They have a meal together, silent while the maid who served them was present, "as a young couple who, on their wedding-journey, at the inn, feel shy in the presence of the waiter" (81). It is as though, at last, her fantasy of love and marriage to the Master has become reality. They discuss the solitude in which they find themselves, and he comments, as maturely as ever, on her special loneliness, a governess's loneliness, but particularly an abandoned governess's loneliness: "Nothing could be more charming than the way you take it, for of course, if we're alone together now it's you that are alone most." She admits that she has stayed on simply for him, though she says, "I've renounced all claims to your company – you're so beyond me – I at least greatly enjoy it. What else should I stay on for?" (83).

But he is wary, and when she repeats that there is nothing she won't do for him – he observes that she only wants to make him tell her something – *that* is what she has stayed on for. Her pressure is extreme; she accuses him of having taken and opened her letter to the Master, embraces him as he admits this, asks him, finally, to confess what he had done at school, and extracts only the pitiful admission that he had "said things." And all the while she sees the face of Quint at the window; challenging Miles to see what she does, she holds him more tightly, "it may be imagined with what a passion." But the last comes. "We were alone with the quiet day, and his little heart, dispossessed, had stopped" (87), released from Quint's "possession."

The ending returns us to the gothic mode that has all along been part of James's design. But it does not reduce the story to a tale of demonic possession. Possession, after all, is another way of describing the mystery of multiple identity – and my argument that the Master and Quint and Miles are one and the Governess, Miss Jessel, and Flora are also one is based on the view that James saw the ambiguity in masculine and class hegemony and saw the Governess both as a sympathetic and even valorous person and as one made dangerous to her society by her "status incongruity" and her nostalgia for the lost security of the class into which she had been born. However much she dreams of the *Jane Eyre* ending, it will be denied her, and her longing will put her in peril of greater displacement, debasement, and destruction.

James's doubling imagination, which has split two figures into six, is rooted in society's splintered vision of the Governess. On the one hand his Governess is that guardian of morality, that providential pilgrim whom the early governess novel celebrated. She rises to the sacrifice the godlike Master has demanded of her, trusting herself to hope only for the heavenly reward of his approval. She encounters agents of Satan, who threaten the innocent souls she has been appointed to guard. Perhaps she knows that she cannot be Jane Eyre, who marries the Master, but she can be a female knight battling against Evil, and she embraces this role with joy: "I was there to protect and defend the little creatures in the world the most bereaved and the most loveable. . . . We were cut off, really, together; we were united in our danger. They had nothing but me, and I – well, I had *them*. It was in short a magnificent chance" (28).

She sustains this vision of herself with difficulty, but she sustains it to the end. As her enemy appears to her repeatedly, she grows in courage. "I found myself," she says, after her third encounter with Quint, "magnificently aware of this. I felt in a fierce rigour of confidence, that if I stood my ground a minute I should cease – for the time at least – to have him to reckon with" (41). Her effort to free Miles and Flora from the infernal powers of Quint and Miss Jessel sustains her against all the doubts that the children's sweetness and beauty continue, like enemies, to assail her with. In the end she believes she has saved Miles, if not Flora, saved his soul at the cost of his life, as he "utter[s] the cry of a creature hurled over an abyss" (88) and she believes she has caught him in his fall.

But her doubt of herself is just as evident throughout her narrative. As she wavers in her conviction of the children's secret wickedness, so she wavers in her conviction of her own virtue. When she sees Miss Jessel at the lake, she is desperate for justification: "She was there, so I was justified, she was there, so I was neither cruel nor mad" (71). Trying to extract a confession from Miles she is assailed by a "perverse horror" of her own effort: "For what did it consist of but the obtrusion of the idea of grossness and guilt on a small helpless creature who had been for me a revelation of the possibilities of beautiful intercourse?" (84). When she wrings from him some admission of his misdeeds at school, they seem so trivial that she swings to "the appalling alarm of his being perhaps innocent. It was for the instant confounding and bottomless, for if he *were* innocent what then on earth was I?" (87).

"Cruel and mad" – or pitiful. Despite Douglas's praise the reader will incline to these negative judgments of the Governess. We may say that her self is a divided one. It is no accident that James has her speculate at the outset about the presence at Bly of "an insane, an unmentionable relative kept in unsuspected confinement," as there was at Thornfield. His Governess does not discover a madwoman in an attic at Bly, but she does discover a hidden female presence just the same, the ghost of her broken predecessor, who, like the cruel and mad Bertha Rochester, is a projection of her secret self.

Or we may say that James presents the Governess in the double vision of the society he knew. He sees her as that society preferred to view her, as a defender of innocence and conserver of morality.

He also sees her as a problematic person whose situation inspires the fear that she will menace the definition of class and gender. Filled with pitiable and dangerous emotions of regret and longing, threatening, by her own possible degradation, the security of the accepted idea of the female self, she becomes a suspect figure. But by doubling his presentation of the Master James makes his tale more daringly subversive of the claims to admiration of masculine mastery – glamorous in the figuration of romance but also the tyrannic wielder of power, the insidious destroyer of female self-hood, the nightmarish Quint.[27]

NOTES

1. *The Turn of the Screw,* ed. Robert Kimbrough (New York: W. W. Norton & Company, Inc., 1966), p. 17. All references to James's text will be to this edition.

2. The subject of Victorian governesses has recently been treated in a number of studies based on nineteenth-century sources, for example, M. Jeanne Peterson, "The Victorian Governess: Status Incongruity in the Family and Society," in *Suffer and Be Still: Women in the Victorian Age,* ed. Martha Vicinus (Bloomington, Ind.: Indiana University Press, 1972), pp. 3–19, and Mary Poovey, *Uneven Developments: the Ideological Work of Gender in Mid-Victorian England* (Chicago, Ill.: University of Chicago Press, 1988), pp. 126–63.

3. Jane Austen, *Pride and Prejudice,* ed. Philip Robinson (London: Longman's, 1983), p. 37.

4. There has been some debate among social historians concerning what has been called the "myth" of the idle Victorian woman, but the consensus remains that as the middle-class sense of status established itself in the first half of the century the idle wife and the idle daughter became the rich man's status symbols, though many middle-class women continued to do much of their household work, including the instruction of their children. The argument is summarized by Margaret Bryant in *The Unexpected Revolution: A Study in the History of the Education of Women and Girls in the Nineteenth Century, Studies in Education* (new series) 10 (London, England: University of London Institute of Education, 1979), pp. 28–31.

5. *The Story of The Governesses' Benevolent Institution* (Southwick, Sussex, England: Grange Press, 1962), p. 14 (quoted in Poovey, p. 232).

6. Poovey, *Uneven Developments,* p. 126.

7. Elizabeth Rigby (Lady Eastlake), untitled review of *Vanity Fair, Jane Eyre,* and the 1847 Report of the Governesses' Benevolent Institution, *Quarterly Review* 94 (1848), 176, 184.

8. Eastlake, untitled review, 176.

9. See Peterson, "The Victorian Governess."

10. Eastlake, untitled review, 177.

11. Andrew Combe, *The Principles of Physiology Applied to the Preservation of Health and to the Improvement of Physical and Mental Education,* 7th ed. (New York: Fowler & Wells, 1848), p. 222. The passage from which I have quoted occurs in the course of Combe's discussion of the effect of solitude on mental health, and reads in full:

> It is the weakening and depressing effect upon the brain of the withdrawal of the stimulus necessary for its healthy exercise, which renders solitary confinement so severe a punishment even to the most daring minds; and it is a lower degree of the same cause which renders continuous seclusion from society so injurious to both mental and bodily soundness, and which often renders the situation of governesses one of misery and bad health, even where every kindness is meant to be shown them. In many families, especially in the higher ranks, the governess lives so secluded, that she is as much out of society as if she were placed in solitary confinement. She is too much above the domestics to make companions of them, and too much below her employers to be treated by them either with confidence or as their equal. With feelings as acute, interests as dear as theirs, and a judgment as sound as those of any of the persons who scarcely notice her existence, she is denied every opportunity of gratifying the first or expressing the last, merely because she is "only the governess"; as if governesses were not made of the same flesh and blood, and sent into the world by the same Creator, as their more fortunate employers. It is, I believe, beyond question that much unhappiness, and not infrequently madness itself, are unintentionally caused by this cold and inconsiderate treatment. (p. 222)

> I gratefully owe to William J. Scheick ("A Medical Source for *The Turn of the Screw," Studies in American Fiction,* 19, Autumn, 1991, 217–20) my discovery of Combe and his observations about governesses. Though I would not go so far as to identify the *Physiology* as a source for *The Turn of the Screw,* Combe clearly expresses the common recognition – shared by James – that madness could result from the sufferings of such women.

12. Eastlake, untitled review, 177.

13. Patricia Thomson, *The Victorian Heroine: A Changing Ideal, 1837–1873*

(London and New York: Oxford University Press, 1956), pp. 39–40. See also Katherine West, *Chapter of Governesses: A Study of the Governess in English Fiction, 1800–1949* (London: Cohen and West, 1949). Inga-Stina Ewbank, *Their Proper Sphere: A Study of the Brontë Sisters as Early-Victorian Female Novelists* (Cambridge, Mass.: Harvard University Press, 1966) discusses the relation of novels by Anne, Emily, and Charlotte Brontë, particularly *Agnes Grey* and *Villette* as well as *Jane Eyre,* to the governess tradition. See also Robert A. Colby, *Fiction with a Purpose: Major and Minor Nineteenth-Century Novels* (Bloomington, Ind.: Indiana University Press, 1968), chap. 6, *"Villette:* Lucy Snowe and the Good Governess."

14. James's interest in popular fiction, particularly novels written by women, and its effect on his writing have been explored by William Veeder in *Henry James: The Lessons of the Master* (Chicago: University of Chicago Press, 1975) and by Alfred Habegger in *Henry James and the "Woman Business"* (New York: Cambridge University Press, 1989).

15. Henry James, "The Speech of American Women," *French Writers and American Women,* ed. Peter Buitenhuis (Bradford, Conn.: The Compass Publishing Co., 1960), pp. 43–4. James's essay was originally published in *Harper's Bazaar,* vol. 40–41 (November, 1906–February, 1907).

16. *The Novels and Tales of Henry James,* 24 vols., The New York Edition (New York: Charles Scribner's Sons, 1907–1909), vol. 16, p. 84.

17. *The Works of William Makepeace Thackeray,* 12 vols. (London: Smith, Elder & Co., 1879), vol. 1, *Vanity Fair,* p. 80.

18. James, *Novels and Tales,* vol. 11, p. 16.

19. Jerome Beaty, *"Jane Eyre* and Genre," *Genre* 10 (Winter, 1977), 624.

20. W. R. Greg, "Why are Women Redundant?" *National Review* 15 (1862), 434–60.

21. Quoted by Leon Edel, *Henry James: The Master: 1901–1917* (Philadelphia: J. B. Lippincott Co., 1972), p. 91.

22. That the Master is the children's father is suggested by John Clair, *The Ironic Dimension in the Fiction of Henry James* (Pittsburgh, Penn.: Duquesne University Press, 1965), pp. 37–58.

23. James wrote in the New York Edition preface:

What, in the last analysis, had I to give the sense of? Of their being, the haunting pair, capable, as the phrase is, of everything.... What would *be* then, on reflection, this utmost conceivability – a question to which the answer all admirably came. There is for such a case no eligible *absolute* of the wrong.... Only make the reader's general vi-

sion of evil intense enough, I said to myself . . . and his own experience, his own imagination, his own sympathy (with the children)
and horror (of their false friends) will supply him quite sufficiently
with all the particulars. . . . There is not only from beginning to end
of the matter not an inch of expatiation, but my values are positively
all blanks save so far as an excited horror, a promoted pity, created
expertness – on which punctual effects of strong causes no writer can
ever fail to plume himself – proceed to read into them more or less
fantastic figures. (*Literary Criticism: French Writers, Other European
Writers, The Prefaces to the New York Edition* [New York: The Library
of America, 1984], p. 1188).

24. Richard Ellmann, "A Late Victorian Love Affair," *The New York Review
of Books* (Aug. 4, 1977), 6–7.

25. See Bruce Robbins, "Shooting Off James's Blanks: Theory, Politics,
and *The Turn of the Screw*," *The Henry James Review* 5, no. 3 (Spring
1984), 193–9.

26. In a radio symposium in 1942, Katherine Anne Porter, Allen Tate,
and Mark Van Doren agreed that Quint has "all the physical attributes
of the legendary devil." *A Casebook on Henry James's "The Turn of the
Screw,"* ed. Gerald Willen (New York: Thomas Y. Crowell Co., 1934),
pp. 163–4.

27. My interpretation of *The Turn of the Screw*, given here, is the latest
stage of an evolving response; readers may be interested in noting
this development for what it illustrates about the way one critic's
interest grows and shifts, perhaps in response to personal as well as
cultural changes. An earlier essay of mine, " 'The Turn of the Screw,'
and the Recherche de l'Absolu" (*Henry James: Fiction as History*, ed.
Ian F. A. Bell [London: Vision and Barnes and Noble, 1984], pp. 65–
81), asserted the "seriousness" of James's intention, despite his own
disclaimers and the deprecations of later criticism. I noted, then, the
pattern of character doubling in the story and the oscillating drama
of the Governess's search for the truth about the children. I connected
these to the Governess's Manichean vision of divided good and evil
and to a philosophical theme, the search for an "absolute" of moral
certainty.

    In *Meaning in Henry James* (Cambridge, Mass.: Harvard University
Press, 1991, pp. 223–42) I enlarged on these ideas, seeing the Governess's inability to establish certainty as related to James's own
suggestive maintenance of "blanks" in the story. The play of inter-
textual reference to *Jane Eyre* exhibits, I discovered, the Governess's
failed attempt to impose a narrative of her own on others. Yet this

unrealizable romance is a part of the story's dynamics; it haunts the text, as it haunts her mind. I also saw more clearly the social meaning of these things from a feminist viewpoint. My discussion of *The Turn of the Screw* begins with the statement that, like other stories by James, this one concerns "a middle-class woman of slender means," and I review the evident economic quandary of Isabel Archer and of her friends Madame Merle and Henrietta Stackpole, of Verena Tarrant, and of Fleda Vetch, and others, as well as of the Governess. For these women only marriage is the practical solution to their difficulties as it is the expected narrative outcome of stories about them. I found myself still more aware of the significance of the story's doubling vision as a way of representing the potentiality for both beauty and horror of polarized sexuality.

The present essay expands further most of these ideas. It particularly elaborates the conflicted role in the story not only of the Brontë prototype but of the whole genre of the governess novel, which I had not previously studied. I now find it impossible to read James's remarkable tale without a sense of its historical meaning. To what I perceived before about its themes and design I have tried to add my more recent perceptions of the actualities of class and sex definition in the nineteenth century and the marginal position of governesses. More than ever James's nameless fictional Governess seems to me a significant and moving figure, both exquisite and degraded; more than ever the nameless Master is a gentleman to flutter the heart of any poor girl, and is also his demon alternate.

In the "Other House" of Fiction:
Writing, Authority, and Femininity
in *The Turn of the Screw*

DAVID MCWHIRTER

ALTHOUGH the famous debate about *The Turn of the Screw* – are the ghosts real? or the hallucinations of a mad governess? – has by no means exhausted itself, critics in recent decades have seemed increasingly willing to allow James's narrative something like a fundamental ambiguity, and to accept the premise that James, as one commentator puts it, wanted his readers to experience "a persistent and uncomfortable vibration between the two interpretations."[1] In practice, however, many of these same critics have been unable to resist the impulse to resolve the discomforting uncertainties of James's story. In a widely admired reading, for example, Tzvetan Todorov has argued that *The Turn of the Screw* is an unusually "pure" example of the "fantastic," a genre he defines precisely by the way it leaves readers poised between natural (mad governess) and supernatural (real ghosts) interpretations of events.[2] Yet by incorporating the ambiguity of *The Turn of the Screw* into the stabilizing, regulatory structure of a genre, Todorov in a sense defuses that ambiguity, eliding the source of the text's power: its refusal to be bound by what Jacques Derrida has called "the law of genre." "As soon as genre announces itself," Derrida writes, "one must respect a norm, one must not cross a line of demarcation, one must not risk impurity, anomaly, or monstrosity."[3] *The Turn of the Screw* continues to terrorize readers because it draws us into an anomalous experiential space, keeping us sus-

I wish to thank Howard Marchitell, Mary Ann O'Farrell, and Vivian Pollak for their helpful comments on various drafts of this essay, and to acknowledge the support of the Interdisciplinary Group for Historical Literary Study at Texas A&M University.

121

pended – in suspense – somewhere *in between* the relatively familiar generic categories of ghost story and psychological case study.

Early in the story, when Mrs. Grose identifies Peter Quint on the basis of the governess's description, we are likely to assume we are dealing with real ghosts; but when Mrs. Grose later fails to see Miss Jessel by the lake, we are forced to reconsider, to wonder if the governess hasn't been hallucinating all along, and thus to reinterpret events we thought we had mastered. As many readers have remarked, often with barely concealed frustration, whenever we begin to think we know how to read *The Turn of the Screw* – as soon as we feel, in other words, that we have grasped the generic conventions through which James wants us to read it – the author gives another disorienting turn to the screw. The result is what Shoshana Felman calls "an uncanny reading effect": "whichever way the reader turns, he can but be turned by the text."[4] And although James later described *The Turn of the Screw* as "a piece of ingenuity pure and simple, of cold artistic calculation, an *amusette* to catch those not easily caught,"[5] the disturbing power and intensity of this text, attested to by generations of readers, indicate that it must have been, even for its author, something more than a brilliantly controlled feat of "artistic calculation." Leon Edel may be overstating the case when he asserts that James was "in some kind of abject terror himself" as he wrote *The Turn of the Screw*,[6] but there is considerable circumstantial evidence to suggest that James was in fact experiencing something analogous to the radical uncertainty and suspense he creates for his characters and readers.

Originally published in 1898, *The Turn of the Screw* belongs to James's so-called "experimental phase," the latter half of the decade of the 1890s during which he also published such notoriously ambiguous texts as "The Figure in the Carpet," *What Maisie Knew*, "In the Cage," *The Sacred Fount*, and *The Awkward Age*. Marked by a new frankness about sexual matters, these fictions struck many of his contemporary readers as strange, shocking, and even willfully perverse. But when reviewers of *The Turn of the Screw* attacked it as "repulsive" and "hopelessly evil,"[7] they were probably responding most essentially to the way in which the story, like the other experimental texts, works to undermine the familiar perspectives, norms, and conventions of literary realism. One of the reasons why critics have continued to argue so passionately about the genre of *The Turn of the Screw* is, I think, that they are also arguing in a more general sense about its fundamental nature or mode: Should we read it as we would, say, *A Christmas Carol* or Hawthorne's tales, in the broad context of nineteenth-century realism? or is it best understood in the context of a self-consciously modern "fantastic" text like Kafka's *The Metamorphosis?* The late 1890s might well be called James's own "awkward age," for all his texts of that period, including *The Turn of the Screw,* are oddly suspended between the traditional realism of his earlier work and the fully elaborated modernism of the *The Ambassadors, The Wings of the Dove,* and *The Golden Bowl,* the "major phase" novels he published in the first years of the new century. James was, moreover, "between" audiences during these years. Increasingly aware that he had lost favor with the mass audience that had made *Daisy Miller* a best-seller, James had attempted, in the early 1890s, to regain his popularity by abandoning fiction and writing for the theater. The results were disastrous: James, famously, was hooted off the stage on the opening night of the play (*Guy Domville* [1895]) he thought his best. When he returned to writing fiction, his experimentation was in part an effort to find and cultivate a new, more specialized community of readers for his work.

"We live notoriously," James would write in his preface to *The Awkward Age,* "in an 'epoch of transition' " (*AN,* 103). And the James of these years is unmistakably a writer in transition, consciously engaged in disrupting the narrative conventions and teleology that had informed a book like *The Portrait of a Lady,* yet often palpably uncertain about the uncharted territory into which these oddly dislocated and dislocating texts seemed to be leading him. James often talked about his fictions from this period as if they had a mysterious and unpredictable will of their own. Indeed, it seems likely, at least in certain instances, that he literally did not know, when he began writing them, where or how they might end, or even *if* they would end. "I remember," he wrote to W. D. Howells, "how I would have 'chucked' *The Sacred Fount* at the fifteenth thousand word, if in the first place I could have afforded to 'waste' 15,000, and if in the second I were not always ridden by a superstitious terror of not finishing." When James, in the same letter, "ruefully and blushingly" explains that *The Sacred Fount,* "like *The Spoils of Poynton, What Maisie Knew,* 'The Turn of the Screw,' and various others," had grown "by a rank force of its own into something of which the idea had, modestly, never been to be a book," he is admitting that his own authorial intentions and power have been suspended, that he himself, like his readers, is being "turned" or *written by* the very texts he is writing.[8]

In his New York Edition prefaces and elsewhere, James repeatedly describes his compositional practice as a conscious compromise between two opposing impulses, the conflicting imperatives of what I will call the *writer* and the *author.* On the one hand James wants, as a *writer,* to foster "the expansive, the explosive principle in [his] material," to allow his texts to develop freely, without a priori restrictions, in any and all directions that the processes of writing might lead; on the other hand, as the *author,* he feels the need to contain the improvisatory, potentially infinite expansiveness of his own writing, to control "the explosive principle" of his fictional "germs" within a limited and limiting narrative frame or design. "Any real art of representation," James insists, is "a controlled and guarded acceptance, in fact a perfect economic mastery, of that conflict" (*AN,* 278). In the experimental fictions, however, this "mastery" gives way to a situation in which the *writer* – the principle of undetermined and uncontrollable growth – seems to have gained the upper hand.[9] A story like *The Turn of the Screw* thus puts in suspense James's own authority, his power as the *author* to determine the shape of his narratives in conformity with his own foreknowledge and intentions. The experimental texts disrupt the paternal metaphor or "myth of filiation" according to which, in Roland Barthes's formulation, "the author is regarded as the father and owner of his work"; what we get instead is a kind of "text" which "is read" – and written – "without the father's signature" or "guarantee," and where the author's presence in the text is therefore "no longer privileged and paternal, the locus of genuine truth, but rather, ludic."[10]

But where Barthes, like other poststructuralist theorists, unhesitatingly valorizes the collapse of the paternal metaphor as a liberation of the writer into a space of free textual play,[11] James, it seems clear, is not so sure. Perhaps because he felt in some way dispossessed of his rightful power over these texts he tended, when pressed by impatient readers to explain their baffling ambiguities, to disown them as minor works, mere experiments. *The Sacred Fount* is thus dismissed as "fanciful, fantastic," and "insubstantial," "the merest of *jeux d'esprit*": "I say it really in all sincerity – the book isn't worth discussing."[12] Similarly, he apologetically describes *The Turn of the Screw* as a "wanton little tale," "shameless" and "inferior," at best a charming "*amusette*," at worst "a poor little pot-boiling story of nothing at all" that he can "only rather blush to see real substance read into."[13] James's comments undoubtedly reflect an understandable authorial reticence; but they also embody a genuine uncertainty about the substance, stature, and value of these texts, an uncertainty that is perhaps best summarized by the title he gave to the volume of short stories he published in 1896: *Embarrassments*.

During the last years of the nineteenth century, James worked almost exclusively in shorter fictional forms, especially the tale and, as in *The Turn of the Screw*, the *nouvelle*; even the longer novels from this period (*What Maisie Knew* and *The Awkward Age*) are slim by his standards. And his tendency to denigrate these fictions reflects in part his often-expressed conviction that his full-length novels constituted his main achievement. Responding in 1913 to a "delightful young man from Texas" who had sought his guidance in approaching the Jamesian canon, James provided two lists, one "elementary," the other more "advanced," of his novels – none of them, it is worth noting, dating from the experimental phase. "When it comes to the shorter Tales," he went on to remark, "the question is more difficult. . . . Come to me about that, dear young man from Texas, later on – you shall have your little tarts when you have eaten your beef and potatoes."[14] *The Turn of the Screw* is undoubtedly something more than a "little tart"; but it is still, in James's view, only a *nouvelle*, a diminutive novel that can hardly be mistaken for "beef and potatoes." Moreover, the feminine ending of the word *nouvelle* adumbrates another aspect of James's uncertainty and "embarrassment" regarding the experimental texts in general, and *The Turn of the Screw* in particular: his sense, as the subtly but surely gendered language of his dismissive comments reveals, that these fictions were slight affairs because they were implicitly "feminized." As a "wanton little text" that shamelessly disregards normal generic categories, *The Turn of the Screw* is something of a "loose cannon" in the Jamesian *oeuvre;* but it is also, I believe, a "loose woman," for the suspense – or was it an abdication? – of the paternal author's "guarantee" involves as well an unsettling suspense of the male author's "normal" or "natural" gender affiliation.

In his biography of James, Leon Edel argues that the experimental phase, especially the sequence of texts that includes *The Other House, What Maisie Knew, The Turn of the Screw,* "In the Cage," and *The Awkward Age,* embodies a process of "imaginative self-therapy" through which the novelist assumed "the safety-disguise of a little girl" in order to work out unresolved psychological tensions, particularly his uncertainties about his own masculinity. For Edel, James's decision to take on "the disguise of femininity" – his imaginative investment in the series of little girls and young women that begins with four-year-old Effie of *The Other House* and ends with eighteen-year-old Nanda Brookenham of *The Awkward Age* – is a reaction to the humiliating failure of his attempt to write for the theater, a failure that inevitably triggered the novelist's lifelong feelings of inadequate or "threatened masculinity." *The Turn of the Screw* occupies a central place in this scheme, for as Edel stresses, it includes "the one little boy in the series," ten-year-old Miles, whose "strong will to masculinity" is not only threatened but destroyed by the "Medea-like" figure of the Governess: "in James's world," Edel concludes, "little boys died. It was safer to be a little girl."[15]

Henry James was a sexually ambivalent man, probably homo-erotically inclined, who grew up in a family where he was often assigned the role of "sissy," and in a society that defined his very vocation as part of a feminized cultural sphere. Unable, as Alfred Habegger has persuasively argued, "to achieve manhood in the culture where he passed his youth and most of his boyhood,"[16] James could not help "feeling that as a boy [he] showed more poorly than girls" – a "weakness of position"[17] he continually projected and explored, not only in his passive, "feminized" male characters, but also in his female protagonists, including the girls and young women of his "awkward age." James's sense of the awkwardness of his sexual position is evident in his preface to the New York Edition volume containing *Daisy Miller,* where he recalls his acute embarrassment as a young American man cut off from the sphere of "serious male interest" – the "downtown" New York world of masculine business activity. If "downtown was," as James writes, "the major key" of American life, then "up-town" – the world of "music-masters and French pastry-cooks," of "ladies and children" and aspiring young novelists – was "the minor." "Banished" from what he calls "the true pasture," James inhabited a feminized cultural and literary realm, symbolized here, intriguingly, by the decidedly "up-town" genre of "the loved *nouvelle* form":

> To ride the *nouvelle* downtown, to prance and curvet and caracole with it there – that would have been the true ecstasy. But a single "spill" – such as I so easily might have had in Wall Street or wherever – would have forbidden me, for very shame, in the eyes of the expert and the knowing, ever to mount again; so that in short it wasn't to be risked on any terms. (*AN,* 272–4)

The pattern of "feminine disguise" Edel discerns in James's experimental texts is crucial to any full understanding of the novelist's work during the late 1890s. But while Edel is surely right to recognize a "threatened masculinity" behind James's "disguise of femininity," the story he tells is basically a familiar one – too familiar, I think – of crisis followed by resolution: the "self-analysis" enacted in the experimental phase leads, "after a period of crisis," to "restored . . . creative power," and to the renewed, remasculinized mastery of the major phase.[18] Edel thus contains James's potentially transgressive immersion in the feminine by seeing in it only a "safe" pathway to a restored, essentially unchanged masculinity, just as other critics have defused the power of the formal and generic dislocations of the experimental phase by seeing in them only a process through which James masters the style and techniques of his major phase.[19] If James's masculinity is threatened, in other words, masculinity itself is not, for Edel unhesitatingly accepts the conventional division of gender (masculine/feminine) and the terms – especially the oedipal terms – through which our culture structures gendered identities, as fixed,

127

unalterable, and "natural." What happens, however, if we resist, at least for the moment, the impulse to read the experimental phase proleptically, as merely a stage in a resolving master narrative of James's career, and instead allow ourselves to experience the full power of the suspense of knowledge, authority, genre, and gender enacted in these texts? What happens if we understand James's "spiritual transvestitism"[20] not as a "safety disguise," but as a genuine experiment in which normative gender constructions are truly at risk?

Derrida argues that certain modern texts, insofar as they violate the law that prohibits the "mixing of literary genres," also pose a threat to the law of "sexual difference between the feminine and masculine genre/gender."[21] When he uses the words "masculine" and "feminine," Derrida is referring not to men and women in a biological sense, but to the meanings, values, and subject positions – concepts like "downtown" and "uptown" – that our culture has coded as "masculine" or "feminine." Barthes's "paternal metaphor" for traditional literary authority both exemplifies and exposes the way in which Western, patriarchal culture tends to associate control, reason, order, structure, and authority with the masculine, while labeling as feminine those qualities – passivity, emotion, disorder, madness, nature – that threaten or cannot be accommodated by existing forms of power. For Barthes and Derrida, however, the distinctively modern (or, as we would say in America, postmodern) text, by suspending the author's "paternity," inevitably brings these feminine elements into play in ways that are disturbing but also potentially productive. Alice Jardine has coined the term *gynesis* to describe this "putting into discourse of 'woman' as that *process* ... intrinsic to the condition of modernity; indeed, the valorization of the feminine, woman, and her obligatory, that is, historical connotations, as somehow intrinsic to new and necessary modes of thinking, writing, speaking."[22] When the law of genre, and the paternal or masculine authority that underwrites the limits, norms, and interdictions of genre, are suspended, the result is a kind of text where, in Derrida's words, "the masculine genre" is subjected to "a random drift that could always render it other."[23]

The Turn of the Screw is, I believe, just such a text, for it engulfs

128

its author as well as its readers in an anomalous narrative space where the "reading effect" analyzed by Felman is inextricably mixed up with the "woman-effect" described by Jardine, and where the suspense of genre coincides with a simultaneously threatening and liberating suspense of gender.[24] The possibility of such a sexual/textual reading finds support in James's critical writings, especially the New York Edition prefaces, where he habitually portrays the *writer/author* opposition described above as a *gendered* conflict of narrative values. In his prefaces, James regularly draws on images associated with femininity – figures of weaving and embroidery, of housewifery, mothering, and nursing – to define those aspects of his art he associates with the *writer*. As "a young embroiderer of the canvas of life," for example, James "work[s] in terror . . . of the tendency inherent in his many-coloured flowers and figures to cover and consume as many as possible of the little holes"; "the prime effect of so sustained a system, so prepared a surface, is to lead on and on" (*AN*, 5–6). The *writer* is a maternal function that protects the free expansion of the text, or a gardener "cultivating . . . possible relations and extensions," "fostering . . . complications almost beyond reckoning" (*AN*, 101). Just as consistently, however, James offers another set of images, drawn from such conventionally masculine spheres as business, architecture, government, war, and law, that figure the paternal mastery of the *author*. The novelist so conceived is "the chief accountant" of his text, or again a "builder," who "places, after an earnest survey, the piers of his bridge," and who works to ensure that his characters provide "sufficiently solid *blocks* of wrought material . . . as to have weight and mass and carrying power" (*AN*, 312, 296–7). If the *writer* is a nurturing mother, the *author* is a father, the possessor of the "majesty of . . . authorship," the originator of "a series of exquisite laws" which govern, shape, and control his works (*AN*, 328): The Jamesian "house of fiction" is both "a literary monument" and a domestic, which is to say culturally feminized, space (*AN*, 48, 52).[25] James typically identifies the "real fascinations" of his art with those processes he sees as feminine: the protection of the fictional seed or "*idée-mère*" (*AN*, 101) from a priori formal, ethical, or epistemological assumptions (from the "laws" of the author/father); the conception of character "*en dis-*

ponibilité" (*AN*, 44), free from the constraints of plot and the threat of paternally determined closure; and the high valuation of details, apart from their function in larger structural or symbolic schemes. But in James's textual practice, the feminine *writer* is invariably opposed, and usually contained, by the masculine *author*, who locates the value of "germs," characters, and details within larger ideological, moral, and aesthetic structures and hierarchies.

In his preface to *The Turn of The Screw*, James depicts the *writer's* "improvisation, the running on and on of invention," as a "stream [that] breaks bounds and gets into flood. Then the waters may spread indeed . . . violating by the same stroke our sense of the course and the channel, which is our sense of the uses of a stream and the virtue of a story." The problem presented by this particular text, James says, was how "to improvise with extreme freedom and yet at the same time . . . without the hint of a flood" – how, in other words, to effect the *writer/author* compromise in a text that, as a "romance" or a "fairy-tale," "wouldn't be thinkable except as free and wouldn't be amusing except as controlled." But as James admits, what he is trying to "control" here is "an excursion into chaos" (*AN*, 171–2). The image of "the stream break[ing] bounds and get[ting] into flood" points to a particularly powerful manifestation of the feminine in *The Turn of the Screw*, for in choosing to present his story through a first-person narrator, James adopts a technique that he elsewhere describes as opening the floodgates to a "terrible *fluidity* of self-revelation" (*AN*, 321 [James's emphasis]). For James, "the romantic privilege of the 'first person'" leads to "the darkest abyss of romance"; it is "a form foredoomed to looseness," and "that looseness," he insists, "was never much my affair" (*AN*, 320). As an extended first-person narrative in which he "cast [his] lot with pure romance" (*AN*, 175), however, *The Turn of the Screw* is clearly *not* James's usual affair. It is also one of a small handful of texts in which the first person in question is a woman – an unusual fact James emphasizes when he notes in his preface that the Governess "has 'authority,' which is a good deal to have given her" (*AN*, 174).[26] For James, the most unsettling anomaly in this text made up of "intense anomalies and obscurities" (*AN*, 173) lies in its oxymoronic conjunction of "woman" and "authority." *The Turn of the Screw* embodies a narrative structure governed by what its author understands to be a deeply astructural principle. For as I have already suggested, an ''authorized femininity'' is in some sense, for James, an impossibility: What is authorized is the absence of authority, what is empowered is a culturally inscribed position (''woman'') of powerlessness.[27] The *author* who enters ''the darkest abyss of romance'' is thus rendered other, becomes a *writer* immersed in the ''terrible fluidity'' of the feminine.

When James remarks on the oddity of the Governess's authority, he is referring not only to her narrative authority, but also to her position in the household at Bly. Dispatched by ''the Master'' (the children's uncle) to ''his other house,'' the Governess exercises ''supreme authority'' over Miles, Flora, and the other servants (5). But her ''sense of property'' (15) and power are constantly threatened, not only by the ghosts who seek to wrest control of the children from her, but also by her own doubts about the legitimacy of her authority, especially in relation to Miles, whom she recognizes as possessing ''a title to independence, the rights of his sex and situation'' (54). From the first, the Governess is acutely aware of the ambiguous nature of her authority. *As* a governess, she occupies a particularly slippery class and gender ''situation'' in the Victorian society which provides the setting for *The Turn of the Screw*. She is, as the Victorians would say, an ''odd woman.'' ''Privately bred'' yet publicly professional, simultaneously a gentlewoman and a servant, the Governess is in charge of children who are socially and, in the case of Miles, sexually, her superiors. Her very existence thus exposes the arbitrariness of the structures and categories – the class, social, and sexual ''genres,'' if you will – which regulate her society and which she is charged with upholding and perpetuating through the education of the young.

Authority must originate somewhere, and in the Governess's case it originates with the children's uncle. But this ''Master'' strangely conditions her employment *and* her authority on her agreement never to ''trouble him – but never, never: neither appeal nor complain nor write about anything; only meet all questions herself'' (6). She is thus left with no recourse of appeal to the source from which her power derives, a ''situation'' the impossibility of which becomes all too clear within hours of her arrival at Bly when the headmaster's letter dismissing Miles from school arrives enclosed in a note from the uncle: " 'Read him please; deal with him; but mind you don't report. Not a word. I'm off' " (10)! The Governess postpones "dealing with" the question of Miles's schooling because the only way she can deal with it is expressly forbidden by the terms of her contract with the uncle. Like Vladimir and Estragon in *Waiting for Godot,* or the hapless K. in Kafka's *The Castle,* she must somehow "meet all questions herself" in a world "governed" by a kind of *deus absconditus* – a "Master" who cannot or will not exercise the authority to which he, at least, would seem to be unambiguously entitled. Given this peculiar set of circumstances – a situation of "great awkwardness" (5), further compounded by the fact that the Governess was, as she tells Mrs. Grose, romantically "carried away" by the uncle in London (9) – it is hardly surprising that she feels herself, within hours of her arrival at Bly, to be "strangely at the helm" of "a great drifting ship" (10). Just as the Jamesian *author* tries to channel and direct the uncontrollable currents of his *writing,* so the Governess attempts to turn the wheel of a ship that is itself turned by a spreading floodtide of experience.

"What I look back upon with amazement," the Governess writes in retrospect, "is the situation I accepted" (14). And the ambiguities of that situation are mirrored in the *mise en abyme* structure of James's text, where questions of authority and "possession" are raised once again. For the Governess's written record of the events at Bly is framed within the story told by Douglas, who reads her story and quite literally owns her manuscript; his story is in turn framed within the narrative of the unnamed "I" of the opening pages, who inherits the Governess's manuscript when Douglas dies. James may well be attempting to contain his own investment in the feminine here, to regulate the "terrible fluidity" of the first person and so readjust the balance between *writer* and *author.* Yet Douglas's authority is itself problematized by the fact that he was secretly in love with the Governess, just as the Governess was "carried away" by the uncle. When asked for the "title" to his story, Douglas replies, " 'I haven't one,' " thus recapitulating her lack of entitlement (6). Moreover, as a few critics have noticed, the narrator of the broader frame story is never explicitly identified as male; we only know that the narrator is on intimate terms with Douglas, and that Douglas thinks him/her a particularly appropriate auditor for this tale.[28]

The most important thing about these frames is that they are conspicuously *not* reasserted at the end of *The Turn of the Screw*. However we are inclined to read the conclusion – has the Governess successfully "dispossessed" Miles, and if so from (or of) what? has she liberated the little boy, or only killed him? – the Governess has the last, albeit deeply indeterminate, word. And just as "the last story" told on the opening night when Douglas reveals his possession of the Governess's tale remains "incomplete and like the mere opening of a serial" (3), so James's text eludes any final possession or understanding by its characters (the frame narrator, Douglas, the Governess herself), its readers, or its author. René Girard has argued that the greatest novels end in "a successful effort to overcome the inability to conclude."[29] James's text, in contrast, embodies the "terror of not finishing" described in his letter to Howells; for like the legendary serpent with its tail in its mouth, *The Turn of the Screw* "ends" by circling back to its beginning, thus leaving us enwound in an endless spiral of speculation and interpretation. In Girard's decidedly masculine, phallogocentric formulation, the conclusion is "the stationary axle around which the wheel of the novel turns," the privileged locus of the *author*'s truth.[30] But in *The Turn of the Screw*, the only such axle is an absence, a lack – in James's terms, a *writer*, or a woman. Hence the "conclusion," far from being "stationary," is only another "turn," another plunge into "a darker obscure" that the Governess, like her creator, experiences as "confounding and bottomless" (87).

The Turn of the Screw is thus another kind of text, and its truth must be sought not in any resolving conclusion, but in the perpetual crises of perception, knowledge, and authority that define its essential rhythm. As we have seen, a deep uncertainty about her own status is part of the baggage the Governess carries with her when she descends from the "bumping swinging coach" (7) to assume her problematical position at Bly. This uncertainty, reinforced by the headmaster's disturbing letter, quickly becomes, once the ghosts begin to appear, a dizzying, "monstrous ordeal"

(80), a perpetual struggle to stabilize her situation, justify herself, and reassert her authority over Flora and Miles in the face of the "monstrous intrusion[s]" of "the others, the outsiders" (53). Just before Quint's first apparition, the Governess describes her desire to protect the children from "the rough future," to provide them, as well as herself, with an existence that is "fenced about and ordered and arranged." But this "romantic" and "royal extension of the garden and the park" is "suddenly broke[n] into" by the appearance of the "unknown man" on the tower: "the change," she writes, "was actually like the spring of a beast" (15). As we might expect, the Governess reacts to this "bewilderment of vision" by seeking an explanation for what has happened; and if she is at first frightened enough to wonder whether there is "a 'secret' at Bly – a mystery of Udolpho or an insane, an unmentionable relative kept in unsuspected confinement" (17) – she soon accounts for the "intrusion" in a more prosaic fashion: The "outsider," she concludes, apparently after making some inquiries in the nearby village, was probably an indiscreet, "unscrupulous traveller, curious in old houses. . . . The good thing, after all, was that we should surely see no more of him" (19).[31]

Although the Governess obviously has romantic tendencies, and has probably read too many gothic novels, there is really nothing remarkable about her response to this first apparition. Like any mature person confronted with a disturbing, unexpected occurrence, she takes in new facts, and then readjusts her position, redrawing ever so slightly the boundaries – the fences, orders, and arrangements – that have previously defined her interpretive framework, to incorporate something that has challenged that framework from outside. The process is repeated some weeks later when the Governess sees the same "stranger" looking in at her through the dining room window. This second encounter is bound to be more disturbing than the first, for it immediately invalidates the conclusion she had reached – "we should surely see no more of him" – and so requires a more radical conceptual readjustment. Instead of keeping the matter to herself, as she did earlier, the Governess now decides that she must bring Mrs. Grose into the situation. Once she has learned or, as some critics would have it, extorted the stranger's identity from the housekeeper,[32] she is quickly overwhelmed by a flood of new information: that Quint had previously been in charge of the household; that in that capacity he had been '' 'much too free' '' with Miles; that ''there had been matters in [Quint's] life, strange passages and perils, secret disorders, vices more than suspected''; and, most unsettling of all, that '' 'Mr. Quint's dead' '' (24–8). Nevertheless, the Governess manages to recapitulate her earlier process of adjustment by once again taking in the ''disorders'' and ''perils'' that come to her from outside – a pattern reflected in her instinctive attempt to incorporate Quint's perspective into her own by ''plac[ing her]self where he had stood'' at the window (21). The Governess, in other words, once more redraws and ''justifies'' her frame of reference to include the new facts which have intruded upon it. Concluding that Quint is real and that he '' 'wants to appear to [the children],' '' she redefines her authority as well, now determining that she will position herself as a ''screen'' in order to ''guard the tranquility'' of the household ''by accepting, by inviting . . . it all'' (26–8).

Whether we understand Quint to be real or a projection of the Governess's imagination, the fundamental nature of her experience, and hence of our own experience as readers, remains one of perpetual crisis: There are always more invasions and intrusions to ''accept'' and ''invite.'' Thus the Governess's newly drawn lines of defense and authority are quickly breached when yet another ''alien object'' (29) appears across the lake in the form of Miss Jessel. Now she must take in not only ''another person'' (45) – the prodigious fact of a second, female ghost – but new facts about Miss Jessel's relationship with Quint, and new questions about the children's knowledge of their intimacy. ''Obliged to re-investigate'' the happenings by the lake, the Governess must moreover incorporate the previously ''inconceivable'' idea that Flora's ''communion'' with Miss Jessel ''must have been for both parties a matter of habit,'' must now include the possibility that the children are already ''lost,'' that '' 'the four,' '' as she tells Mrs. Grose, '' 'perpetually meet' '' (33, 35, 48). This rhythm of intrusion, inclusion, and readjustment – this ongoing process of conceiving the previously inconceivable – only accelerates as the Governess is exposed to ''constant fresh discoveries'' (19) that she in turn must incorporate into her ever-expanding conceptual framework. Repeatedly she thinks she has touched bottom only to find that "deeper depths of consternation . . . had opened beneath [her] feet" (74); again and again she believes she has finally "piece[d] it all together" (49) through her "pensive embroidery" (39), only to discover another loose thread that must be woven in or to catch another disorienting "view of the back of the tapestry" (46). Thus when Miss Jessel appears by the lake for the second time, the Governess feels – as she does on so many other occasions – that "the whole thing" is at last within her grasp, that she is once and for all "justified," only to have her "situation horribly crumble" when Mrs. Grose fails to see the ghost: "into [the Governess's] attitude Mrs. Grose immediately and violently entered, breaking." Yet even amidst her "sense of ruin," the Governess is already "tak[ing] the measure . . . of what [she] should have from this instant to deal with" (71–2). Once again she begins to reconstruct her situation by expanding it, by including within its parameters "still other things" (48), by taking in what she has previously designated as existing outside the realm of possibility.

Like the Jamesian *writer*, the Governess practices a form of improvisatory authority that instinctively moves toward incorporation rather than exclusion of the other: Always open to "the abrupt transformation of [her] office" (79), she is seemingly unwilling or unable to restrict the potentially infinite proliferation of meanings by adhering rigidly to any preconception of her situation, or by pursuing a definitive, determining course of action. This modus operandi bears a striking resemblance to the textual process of "inclusion" or "invagination" described by Derrida, a "feminine" process, he argues, that relentlessly exposes the arbitrariness of "all genres of genre," and of the boundary lines which define and sustain them. "Invagination is the inward refolding of *la gaine* [sheath, girdle], the inverted reapplication of the outer edge to the inside of a form where the outside then opens a pocket."[33] In such a structure, every limit drawn between inside and outside inevitably ruptures and divides, "form[ing], by invagination, a pocket that is larger than the whole," and opening a "floodgate of genre [that] declasses what it allows to be classed," making it "impossible to settle upon the simple borderlines of this corpus [that] unremittingly repeal[s] itself within its own expansion." The result is "an abounding [that] remains as singular as it is limitless," a structure *en abyme* in which the Girardian demand for a conclusive "truth" is, as Derrida puts it, "itself recounted and swept along in the endless process of invagination." Indeed, this process of "inclusion" is by definition "interminable," for it "can only turn in circles in an unarrestable, inenarrable, and insatiably recurring manner – but one terrible for those who, in the name of the law, require that order reign in the account."[34]

Seen from the perspective of the masculine demand for "law" and "order . . . in the account," the feminine, invaginated text inevitably becomes a terrible kind of madness. This is, I think, why contemporary reviewers found the Governess's story "repulsive" and "hopelessly evil"; it is also why Edel, with his rigid adherence to the law of sexual difference, focuses his reading of *The Turn of the Screw* – a story he tells us is the centerpiece in a sequence of studies of girls and young women – almost exclusively on the threatened masculinity of a little boy. Edel's unwillingness to question the meanings of masculinity and femininity in a text that deliberately puts those meanings in suspense leads him to privilege what he takes to be the conclusion of James's tale – Miles's death – as the locus of its truth. The Governess, in this reading, "becomes the devil," the other; by objectifying her as the mad destroyer of Miles's "will to masculinity" and the agent of his castration, Edel in effect writes the processes of her subjectivity – the very substance of the narrative – *out* of the story. James was undoubtedly expressing some of his deepest anxieties through his identification with Miles, but *The Turn of the Screw* as we experience it is most essentially the Governess's story, *her* account of *her* own experience, and Edel never really asks what James was expressing through his imaginative investment *in* her.

There can be little doubt that the Governess's unlimited responsiveness, her willingness always to take in more and still more, at some point becomes a formula for moral and psychological vertigo, in effect a kind of hysteria, where any possibility of a stable identity or authority collapses, overwhelmed by the sheer volume of the spreading flood that no channel, however broad or deep, can succeed in containing: The "cup . . . held high and full to the brim" through which she figures her experience repeatedly "overflow[s]

137

in a deluge" (70) she cannot control. Yet as Derrida argues, the madness of invagination also carries the potential to undo "the madness of genre," to "repeal" or destabilize the law that requires order, that always establishes "order" by excluding or repressing the other through the establishment of rigid boundaries between inside and outside. Diana Fuss has shown how the figure inside/ outside functions in our culture as the very basis of signification and meaning production. "It has everything to do with the structures of alienation, splitting, and identification which together produce a self and an other, a subject and an object, an unconscious and a conscious, an interiority and an exteriority" – that is, with the psychic and cultural processes that produce identity, and specifically gendered identity. Thus "the figure inside/outside, which encapsulates the structure of language, repression, and [normative] subjectivity, also designates the structure of exclusion, oppression, and repudiation."[35] In this light, the Governess's seemingly endless capacity for adjusting and readjusting the boundary lines that define her position might be seen as embodying a healthy, albeit subversive, flexibility, a genuinely responsible kind of authority that eschews another, less obvious kind of madness: the paranoid refusal of the inconceivable, the labeling of what exists outside of "normal" or socially sanctioned conceptual boundaries as "mad" – evil, perverted, or illegitimate.

Girard insists that "great novels always spring from an obsession that has been transcended": At the novel's conclusion, the hero "achieves truth and . . . entrusts his creator with the heritage of his clairvoyance."[36] But the Governess's primary legacy to James is an "endless obsession" (62), a continual infolding and repealing of the limits that achieve truth only by dividing it into mutually exclusive terms: truth/error; good/evil; sanity/madness; order/disorder; masculine/feminine. The Governess's account, written years after the occurrence of the events it describes, reveals a subject still enmeshed in the ordeal of attempting to formulate and justify her interpretation of those events, still engaged in the process of attempting to accommodate and structure the proliferating array of potential significances that continually intrude on and provoke adjustments in her narrative authority even as she tells her story. And James himself, like Douglas, the frame narrator, and the reader, is in effect taken in by her endless process of incorporation and expansion, the invaginated structure of her ambiguous authority which forms a pocket larger than the *authored* whole that contains it. As Felman rightly insists, "there is no place from which [the Governess's] madness can be judged *from the outside*": "*The Turn of the Screw* imposes [her] viewpoint upon us as the rhetorical condition of our perception of the story."[37]

The participation of writer and reader in the invaginating processes of the Governess's experience and of James's text consistently works to deconstruct any reliable boundary between inside and outside, and so to destabilize the binary divisions that structure authority and identity. And at the risk of falling into the "reader-trap" described by Felman – the trap that lures one into believing "that one is on the *outside*, that one *can* be outside"[38] – I want to suggest that James's investment in the Governess, and in the processes of *writing* and feminine textuality more generally, may have allowed him to express and explore his own ambiguous, embarrassed sexual position. As Douglas's opening response to Griffin's story of a "visitation [that] had fallen on a child" – " 'what do you say to *two* children?' " (1) – implies, much of the terror (and the pleasure?) of James's tale derives from its constant doublings and redoublings of the possibilities that can or must be entertained. If there are two children (girl and boy), there are also two ghosts (woman and man), each of whom appears on multiple occasions. The result is a rapidly proliferating array of "evil" permutations. And given James's studied refusal to specify the source or nature of the evil – "my values," he remarks, "are positively all blanks" (*AN,* 177) – it is not surprising that critics have rushed to fill the vacuum with varied speculations about the characters' sexual desires and relations. Where Edmund Wilson once explained – or perhaps explained away – the mysteries at Bly in terms of the Governess's supposedly repressed desire for the Master,[39] recent commentators have suggested that the Governess in fact desires Miles, or that there is an illicit liaison between Miss Jessel and Quint or between Jessel and the Master, or that Miles and Flora have been corrupted by, respectively, Jessel and Quint, or even, as in Richard Ellmann's reading, that the relationships between Quint and Miles and between Jessel and Flora are homosexual.[40]

My purpose here is not to argue the relative merits of these conflicting interpretations – indeed, there is no compelling reason to assume they are mutually exclusive – but to point out how this proliferation of possible sexual desires and positions, all of them illegitimate in normative social terms, is in fact invited – strangely authorized – by James's "feminine" text. It is not simply that James appeals to the reader's "own experience ... own imagination ... own sympathy ... and horror" to "supply ... all the particulars" (*AN*, 176); more important, to be immersed in the Governess's experience is to be radically, endlessly *in between*, adrift in a textual/sexual process where the boundary lines that structure and sanction gendered, sexual identities are repeatedly ruptured and folded back upon themselves. Because her authority – her sense of identity and of reality – is always in crisis, the Governess is acutely aware of what Terry Heller calls "the fictionality" of all authority, of the ways in which self and society dismiss as inconceivable possibilities that have in fact simply been ruled out or excluded as unacceptable. Her ambivalent relationship to her authority, as well as her position as "a woman in a male-dominated society," thus contributes, in Heller's words, to making her " 'privileged' in the sense that she has access to what her society declares invisible. ... She is especially able to point toward aspects of reality that disappear from within the [dominant] Victorian perspective, thus exposing the illusion that it includes all reality."[41]

Yet if James gains, through the Governess, the privilege of imagining and exploring alternative sexual identities, including those "other" masculinities that Edel so blindly excludes, he also inherits from her the "terror of not finishing" embodied in her ceaseless, ever more frantic attempts to redraw the lines of her authority, to reestablish the boundaries between inside and outside, good and evil, truth and error. The very processes that work to rupture the binary divisions that structure language, identity, and culture inevitably reveal and even depend on the persistence of those categories; the deconstruction of genre is inseparable from its law.

In a famous passage from the preface to *Roderick Hudson*, James argued that "really, universally, relations stop nowhere," and that "the exquisite problem of the artist is eternally but to draw, by a geometry of his own, the circle within which they shall happily *appear* to do so" (*AN*, 5). And although the tension framed in this ambiguous statement – is the circle drawn where relations "appear" to stop? or where the appearance that "relations stop nowhere" is successfully rendered? – should remind us that *The Turn of the Screw* is most essentially the representation of an "endless obsession," it also raises the question of why James chose to put a stop to the proliferating relations engendered by his text at the moment of Miles's death. The story's last scene is clearly not a conclusion in the strong Girardian sense. It would be difficult, I think, to anticipate this end at any earlier point in the story, for it does not reflect the kind of teleological necessity that marks, for example, the conclusion of realism's marriage plot – though it is perhaps predictable insofar as it results from a particularly acute manifestation of the Governess's and James's recurrent need to reassert their authority.

More important, however, the decision to terminate *The Turn of the Screw* at this moment – as our focus contracts so tightly in the end on Miles – may tell us something about what was at stake for James in this text. After Flora, somewhat inconsequently, has left for London with Mrs. Grose, the Governess, preparing for what will prove to be her final engagement with Miles, articulates once more her resistance to any binary division of experience:

> Here at present I felt afresh – for I had felt it again and again – how my equilibrium depended on the success of my rigid will, the will to shut my eyes as tight as possible to the truth that what I had to deal with was, revoltingly, against nature. I could only get on at all by taking "nature" into my confidence and my account, by treating my monstrous ordeal as a push in a direction unusual, of course, and unpleasant, but demanding after all, for a fair front, only another turn of the screw of ordinary human virtue. (80)

For the Governess even what appears to be horrifyingly "against nature" must be taken in, included as a part of nature itself. Yet when Miles attempts to articulate the "nature" of the offenses which have caused him to be expelled from school – " 'I said things,' " he explains in "a manner . . . almost helpless," to " 'those I liked' " – the Governess, feeling herself "float[ing] not into clearness, but into a darker obscure," responds with an almost spasmodic grasp at clarity and order: "the white face of damnation" appears once again at the window, causing her to "shriek," " 'No more, no more, no more!' " (86–8) If Miles is attempting to express his homoerotic feelings for the boys he "liked," the Governess's refusal at this moment to take in "more" is more than a willful blindness: It is "a great betrayal" (88), not only of Miles, but of her own experience.

It is significant, too, that Miles, recognizing that the Governess has seen a "visitant" at the window, initially asks, " 'Is she *here?*' " Only after the Governess proclaims that " 'It's not Miss Jessel' " does he bewilderedly wonder, " 'It's *he?*' " The Governess's response – " 'Whom do you mean by 'he'?' " – elicits Miles's "supreme surrender of the name": " 'Peter Quint – you devil!' " It also suggests that Miles's death, described by the Governess as "the cry of a creature hurled over an abyss" (88), is less the destruction of a certain "will to masculinity" at the hands of a castrating woman than the agony of an as yet unfixed sexual identity being forcibly split and bound, in effect "dispossessed," by the law that rules out certain desires as anomalous or "against nature." James's investment in the feminine – his strange visit to this other, ghostly house of fiction – undoubtedly reflects a threatened masculinity. But it is also an attempt to see the invisible, to say the unsayable, an effort to express the experience of in-betweenness for which our language and culture, and all the genres of genre they entail, possess no adequate terms.

NOTES

1. Terry Heller, *The Turn of the Screw: Bewildered Vision* (Boston: Twayne, 1989), p. 15. For some other key readings that emphasize the fundamental ambiguity of James's story, see Shoshana Felman, "Turning the Screw of Interpretation," *Literature and Psychoanalysis. The Question of Reading: Otherwise* (Baltimore: The Johns Hopkins University Press, 1977), pp. 94–207; Charles Thomas Samuels, "Introduction," *The Ambiguity of Henry James* (Urbana: University of Illinois Press, 1971); Kevin Murphy, "The Unfixable Text: Bewilderment of Vision in *The Turn of the Screw*," *Texas Studies in Literature and Language* 20 (Winter 1978): 538–51; Shlomith Rimmon, *The Concept of Ambiguity: The Example of Henry James* (Chicago: University of Chicago Press, 1977),

pp. 116–66; and Christine Brooke-Rose, *A Rhetoric of the Unreal: Studies in Narrative and Structure, Especially of the Fantastic* (Cambridge: Cambridge University Press, 1981), pp. 103–229. For an interesting historicist critique of the tendency to valorize James's ambiguity, see John Carlos Rowe, "Psychoanalytical Significances: The Use and Abuse of Uncertainty in *The Turn of the Screw*," *The Theoretical Dimensions of Henry James* (Madison: University of Wisconsin Press, 1984), pp. 119–46.

2. Tzvetan Todorov, *The Fantastic*, trans. Richard Howard (Ithaca: Cornell University Press, 1973), p. 43.

3. Jacques Derrida, "The Law of Genre," trans. Avital Ronell, *On Narrative*, ed. W. J. T. Mitchell (Chicago: University of Chicago Press, 1981), p. 53.

4. Shoshana Felman, "Turning the Screw of Interpretation," p. 101.

5. The quotation is from James's New York Edition preface to *The Turn of the Screw*, in *The Art of the Novel*, ed. Richard P. Blackmur (New York: Charles Scribner's Sons, 1934), p. 172. All future references to James's prefaces are keyed to Blackmur's volume, hereafter cited parenthetically as *AN*.

6. Leon Edel, *Henry James: The Treacherous Years, 1895–1901* (New York: Avon, 1978), p. 202.

7. Reviews from *The Outlook* 60, October 29, 1898, 537, and *The Independent* 51, January 5, 1899, 73, reprinted in the Norton Critical Edition of *The Turn of the Screw*, ed. Robert Kimbrough (New York: Norton, 1966), pp. 172, 175.

8. Letter of December 11, 1902, in *Henry James Letters*, ed. Leon Edel, vol. 4 (Cambridge: Harvard University Press, 1984), p. 251.

9. I explore the *writer/author* distinction at greater length in *Desire and Love in Henry James: A Study of the Late Novels* (Cambridge: Cambridge University Press, 1989), where I argue that James's last two completed novels (*The Wings of the Dove* and *The Golden Bowl*) embody a renewed ascendance of the *author* over the *writer;* my reading of *The Ambassadors*, in contrast, emphasizes its continuities with the more *writerly* texts of the experimental phase. See especially pages 7–8, 60–3, 92–6, and 159–62.

10. Roland Barthes, "From Work to Text," in *Textual Strategies: Perspectives in Post-Structuralist Criticism*, ed. Josué V. Harari (Ithaca: Cornell University Press, 1979), p. 78.

11. Barthes describes the text as "the space in which no one language has a hold over any other, in which all languages circulate freely" ("From Work to Text," p. 80); also see his related essay, "The Death

of the Author," *The Rustle of Language,* trans. Richard Howard (New York: Farrar, Straus & Giroux, 1986), pp. 49–55. For an overview of the ways in which "the breakdown of the paternal metaphor in Western culture" has led poststructuralist theorists to "valorize other metaphors," especially metaphors associated with the feminine, see Alice Jardine, *Gynesis: Configurations of Women and Modernity* (Ithaca: Cornell University Press, 1985), pp. 27, 65–102.

12. Letter to James B. Pinker, July 25, 1900, *Letters,* vol. 4, p. 154; unpublished letter to Duchess of Sutherland, quoted in Leon Edel, "Introductory Essay" to *The Sacred Fount* (New York: Grove, 1953), p. xxx; letter to Mrs. Humphrey Ward, March 15, 1901, *Letters,* vol. 4, pp. 185–6.

13. Letter to Dr. Louis Waldstein, October 21, 1898; letter to F. W. H. Myers, December 19, 1898, *Letters,* vol. 4, pp. 84, 88; letter to Paul Bourget, August 19, 1898 (in Norton Critical Edition of *The Turn of the Screw,* p. 109); and *AN,* p. 172.

14. Letter to Fanny Prothero, September 14, 1913, *Letters,* vol. 4, pp. 683–4.

15. Edel, *The Treacherous Years,* pp. 261–4; 208–11.

16. Alfred Habegger, *Gender, Fantasy, and Realism in American Literature* (New York: Columbia University Press, 1982), pp. 258–9.

17. Henry James, *Autobiography,* ed. Frederick W. Dupee (Princeton: Princeton University Press, 1983), p. 217.

18. Edel, *The Treacherous Years,* p. 264.

19. See, for example, Robert Kimbrough's preface to the Norton Critical Edition of *The Turn of the Screw,* p. ix.

20. Edel, *The Treacherous Years,* p. 265.

21. Derrida, "The Law of Genre," p. 70.

22. Jardine, *Gynesis,* p. 25.

23. Derrida, "The Law of Genre," p. 72.

24. Jardine, *Gynesis,* p. 28. To say that the James of *The Turn of the Screw* occupies narrative, linguistic, and cultural positions that he, like the society in which he lived, understood as "feminine" is not to suggest that the story is anything like a feminist text. Jardine herself acknowledges that many feminists are likely to see the "woman-effect" valorized by (mostly male) poststructuralist theorists as just another tactic – a strategic appropriation of "woman" – aimed at reinscribing masculine authority. Women's own writing can easily be marginalized by this kind of theory, as when Gilles Deleuze and Félix Guattari remark that Virginia Woolf incorporated the process of what they call "becoming woman" in her writing, but not "to the same extent" as

D. H. Lawrence, Henry Miller, or Henry James, the latter of whom "is swept up in an irresistible becoming-woman" (see Deleuze and Guattari, *A Thousand Plateaus: Capitalism and Schizophrenia,* trans. Brian Massumi [Minneapolis: University of Minnesota Press, 1987], pp. 276–7, 290). Moreover, although James has rightly been praised for his sympathetic portrayals of women, his response to the social and political agendas of contemporary feminist women was quite conservative, at times simply reactionary. Nevertheless, although James, like most people, had deeply internalized his culture's codification of gender, he was also persistently moved to explore and experience the position of the sexual other within his culture and psyche. For background on James's responses to contemporary feminism, see Alfred Habegger, *Henry James and the "Woman Business"* (Cambridge: Cambridge University Press, 1989), especially pages 182–229. My goal here is not to critique James's conception of masculinity and femininity, but to explore what was at stake for him when he wrote, as he did in *The Turn of the Screw,* in a mode he himself understood as feminine.

25. For an extended exploration of the domestic/feminine implications of the house of fiction metaphor, see Sara B. Blair, "In the House of Fiction: Henry James and the Engendering of Literary Mastery," forthcoming in *Henry James and the Construction of Authorship: Essays on The New York Edition,* ed. David McWhirter (Stanford University Press). The interplay of masculine and feminine metaphors is especially striking in James's preface to *The Awkward Age* (*AN,* 98–118), a novel he sees as both a densely detailed and closely textured "tapestry" and a structure, reared on a firm "foundation," produced by his own "master-hammer" (*AN,* 109, 115).

26. In her dissertation in progress, "The Detached 'I' of Henry James: Narrative Technique in the Short Fiction," Doris Helbig of the University of North Carolina at Chapel Hill counts just eight female narrators out of a total of fifty stories that use the first-person technique. These are "Master Eustace," "The Sweetheart of M. Briseux," "Impressions of a Cousin," "The Path of Duty," "The Visits," "The Way It Came," "Maud Evelyn," and *The Turn of the Screw.* It is intriguing that all these stories mirror *The Turn of the Screw* in employing some type of mediating device (letters, diaries, oral frames) to enclose the narrative of the female first person.

In comparing Freud's *A Fragment of an Analysis of a Case of Hysteria* ("Dora") to *The Turn of the Screw,* Paula Cohen stresses the ways in which James's first-person narration – in contrast to Freud's "third-person 'telling' of Dora's case" — allows the novelist, "at least temporarily," to identify with "the governess's case": "James's identification with her becomes a giving up of the safety and seeming sanity of male identification for the solitude and risk of insanity of female identification" ("Freud's *Dora* and James's *The Turn of the Screw*: Two Treatments of the Female 'Case,' " *Criticism* 28 [1986]: 81).

27. James, it is worth emphasizing, identified with and explored this oxymoronic situation — the impossible position of unauthorized authority — throughout his career, from *The Portrait of a Lady* to *The Golden Bowl*. See Millicent Bell's perceptive remark that James "identifies with the female condition simply because it is, more absolutely, the human condition as he sees it" (*Meaning in Henry James* [Cambridge: Harvard University Press, 1991], p. 42).

28. Michael J. H. Taylor sees the frame narrator's sex as deliberately ambiguous ("A Note on the First Narrator of 'The Turn of the Screw,' " *American Literature* 53 [January 1982]: 717–22); Terry Heller (*Bewildered Vision*, p. 21) follows Linda S. Kauffman ("The Author of Our Woe: Virtue Recorded in *The Turn of the Screw*," *Nineteenth-Century Fiction* 36 [1981]: 176–92) in arguing that the unnamed "I" is probably a woman. The main and, I think, less than conclusive piece of evidence supporting the view that the frame narrator is a man lies in his/her remark that "the departing ladies who had said they would stay" for Douglas's reading of the Governess's manuscript "didn't, of course, thank heaven, stay" (4).

29. René Girard, *Deceit, Desire, and the Novel: Self and Other in Literary Structure*, trans. Yvonne Freccero (Baltimore: The Johns Hopkins University Press, 1965), p. 308.

30. Girard, *Deceit, Desire, and the Novel*, p. 307. Derrida would presumably include Girard among those

> authorities who demand an *author*, an *I* capable of organizing a narrative sequence, of remembering and telling the truth: ... in other words [of] saying "I" (I am the same as the one to whom these things happened, and so on, and thereby assuring the unity or identity of the narratee or reader, and so on). Such is the demand for the story, for narrative, the demand that society, the law that governs artistic and literary works, medicine, the police, and so forth, claim to constitute. (Derrida, "Living On: Border Lines," trans. James Hulbert, *Deconstruction and Criticism*, ed. Harold Bloom et al. [New York: Seabury Press, 1979], p. 98).

In terms that contrast suggestively with Girard's emphasis on strong novelistic conclusions, Hélène Cixous describes a "feminine textual body" that can be

> recognized by the fact that it is always endless, without end-
> ing; there's no closure, it doesn't stop, and it's this that very
> often makes the feminine text difficult to read . . . a feminine
> text goes on and on and at a certain moment the volume
> comes to an end but the writing continues and for the reader
> this means being thrust into the void. (Hélène Cixous, "Cas-
> tration or Decapitation?" *Signs* 7 [1981]: 53)

31. When the Governess first tells Mrs. Grose about the man on the tower, the latter wonders whether it might have been someone " 'about the place' " or " 'from the village.' " The Governess's reply – " 'Nobody – nobody. I didn't tell you, but I made sure' " – indicates that she has already made some inquiries on her own.

32. See, for example, Edel's contention that the Governess "leads [Mrs. Grose], by elaborate cross-examination, to pronounce the name of Peter Quint" (*The Treacherous Years*, p. 204).

33. Derrida, "Living On: Borderlines," p. 97.

34. Derrida, "The Law of Genre," pp. 55, 61, 66–7; "Living On: Bor-derlines," 98.

35. Diana Fuss, "Inside/Out," in *Inside/Out: Lesbian Theories, Gay Theories,* ed. Diana Fuss (New York: Routledge, 1991), pp. 1–2.

36. Girard, *Deceit, Desire, and the Novel,* pp. 300, 296.

37. "Turning the Screw of Interpretation," pp. 200–1. Felman also points to the ways in which the narrative frames serve both to pull "the outside of the story into its inside by enclosing in it . . . its own readers," and to pull "the inside outside: for in passing through the echoing chain of the multiple, repetitive narrative voices, it is the very *content,* the *interior* of the story which becomes somehow *exterior to itself,* reported as it is by a voice inherently alien to it and which can render of it but 'the shadow of a shadow.' " The result, as Felman puts it, is "a blurring of the very difference between inside and out-side" (p. 123).

38. Felman, "Turning the Screw of Interpretation," p. 199.

39. Edmund Wilson, "The Ambiguity of Henry James," *A Casebook on Henry James's 'The Turn of the Screw,'* ed. Gerald Willen (New York: Thomas Crowell, 1969), pp. 115–53.

40. Millicent Bell, for example, finds "an intensity we are likely to feel as almost sexual" in the relationship between the Governess and Miles, and suggests the possibility that the children have been "sex-ually initiated by Miss Jessel and Quint" (*Meaning in Henry James,*

pp. 225–6). John Clair argues that the children are the illegitimate offspring of the uncle and Miss Jessel (*The Ironic Dimension in the Fiction of Henry James* [Pittsburgh: Duquesne University Press, 1965], pp. 37–58); John Carlos Rowe suggests that they might be the illegitimate children of the uncle's younger brother and Miss Jessel (*Theoretical Dimensions of Henry James*, p. 134). For Ellmann's reading, see "A Late Victorian Love Affair," *The New York Review*, August 4, 1977: 6–7; Ellmann argues that Miles is expelled from school because of his involvement in homosexual practices. For an overview of the various kinds of sexual corruption Victorian readers would probably have sensed in James's tale, see Elliot M. Schrero, "Exposure in *The Turn of the Screw*," *Modern Philology* 78 (1981): 261–74.

41. Heller, *Bewildered Vision*, pp. 136–7.

Notes on Contributors

Millicent Bell, Professor of English at Boston University, is the author of numerous books and essays on American literature, including *Meaning in Henry James* (1991). Editor of *The Complete Novels of Nathaniel Hawthorne* (1983), she is presently editing James's *Autobiographical Writings*.

Kenneth Graham, formerly Professor of English Literature at the University of Sheffield in England, is currently Professor of English Literature at the University of Neuchâtel, Switzerland. He is the author of *English Criticism of the Novel 1865–1900* (1965); *Henry James: The Drama of Fulfilment* (1975); *Indirections of the Novel: James, Conrad, Forster* (1988); various articles on English and American literature; a novel; and several short stories.

David McWhirter, Associate Professor of English at Texas A & M University, is the author of *Desire and Love in Henry James: A Study of the Late Novels* (1989). He is also the editor of a forthcoming collection of essays on James's New York Edition.

Vivian R. Pollak, Professor of English and Adjunct Professor of Women Studies at the University of Washington in Seattle, is the author of *Dickinson: The Anxiety of Gender* (1984) and editor of *A Poet's Parents: The Courtship Letters of Emily Norcross and Edward Dickinson* (1988). The author of wide-ranging essays and reviews on American literature and culture, she is currently completing a book on *The Erotic Whitman*.

Robert Weisbuch, Professor and Chair of English at the University of Michigan, is the author of two books, *Emily Dickinson's Poetry* (1976) and *Atlantic Double-Cross: American Writers and British Influence in the Age of Emerson* (1986), as well as a number of essays and reviews. His current projects include a history of American radio.

Selected Bibliography

The life and work of Henry James exists within a rich social context and the secondary literature on James reflects this amplitude. First, there is James within the James family, surely one of the most fascinating social organisms ever presented to the eager biographer. Then there is James within the larger literary community. These transatlantic relations with the men and women who were his friends and asociates constitute a veritable gold mine for the literary historian. Himself an avid critic of his own works, of the works of others, and of the art of fiction, James presents an equally abundant range of relations for the literary critic. Though in recent years *Daisy Miller* has received less critical attention than *The Turn of the Screw,* the list that follows includes material relevant for both stories, as well as studies that are more narrowly focused. References to other valuable works may be found in the notes to the essays in this volume.

Biography, autobiography, and literary relations

Edel, Leon. *Henry James: The Untried Years 1843–1870, The Conquest of London 1870–1881, The Middle Years 1882–1895, The Treacherous Years 1895–1901, The Master 1901–1916.* 5 vols. Philadelphia: J. B. Lippincott, 1953–72.

Feinstein, Howard M. *Becoming William James.* Ithaca: Cornell University Press, 1984.

James, Alice. *The Death and Letters of Alice James.* Ed. Ruth Bernard Yeazell. Berkeley: University of California Press, 1981.

The Diary of Alice James. Ed. Leon Edel. New York: Dodd, Mead, 1964.

James, Henry. *Autobiography: A Small Boy and Others, Notes of a Son and Brother, The Middle Years.* Ed. Frederick W. Dupee. Princeton: Princeton University Press, 1983.

Selected Bibliography

Henry James: Letters 1843–1875, Letters 1875–1883, Letters 1883–1895, Letters 1895–1916. Ed. Leon Edel. 4 vols. Cambridge: Harvard University Press, 1974–84.

James, William. *The Letters of William James.* Ed. Henry James III. 2 vols. Boston: Atlantic Monthly Press, 1920.

Kelley, Cornelia Pulsifer. *The Early Development of Henry James.* Urbana: University of Illinois Press, 1965.

LeClair, Robert C. *Young Henry James: 1843–1870.* New York: Bookman Associates, 1955.

Lewis, R. W. B. *The Jameses: A Family Narrative.* New York: Farrar, Straus, & Giroux, 1991.

Maher, Jane. *Biography of Broken Fortunes: Wilkie and Bob, Brothers of William, Henry, and Alice James.* Hamden, Conn.: Archon Books, 1986.

Matthiessen, F. O. *The James Family: Including Selections from the Writings of Henry James, Senior, William, Henry, & Alice James.* New York: Alfred A. Knopf, 1947.

Nowell-Smith, Simon. *The Legend of the Master.* London: Constable, 1947.

Strouse, Jean. *Alice James: A Biography.* Boston: Houghton Mifflin, 1980.

Collections of essays, source materials, and reader's guides

Cranfill, Thomas Mabry and Clark, Robert Lanier, Jr. *An Anatomy of The Turn of the Screw.* Austin: University of Texas Press, 1965.

Fogel, Daniel Mark. *Daisy Miller: A Dark Comedy of Manners.* Boston: Twayne, 1990.

Heller, Terry. *The Turn of the Screw: Bewildered Vision.* Boston: Twayne, 1989.

James, Henry. *Tales of Henry James.* Ed. Christof Wegelin. New York: W. W. Norton, 1984.

  The Turn of the Screw. Ed. Robert Kimbrough. New York: W. W. Norton, 1966.

Sheppard, E. A. *Henry James and The Turn of the Screw.* Auckland University Press-Oxford University Press, 1974.

Stafford, William T. *James's Daisy Miller: The Story, The Play, The Critics.* New York: Scribner's, 1963.

Willen, Gerald. *A Casebook on Henry James's ''The Turn of the Screw.''* New York: Thomas Y. Crowell, 1969. 2d ed.

Criticism

Banta, Martha. *Henry James and the Occult: The Great Extension.* Bloomington: Indiana University Press, 1972.

Beidler, Peter G. *Ghosts, Demons, and Henry James: The Turn of the Screw at the Turn of the Century*. Columbia: University of Missouri Press, 1989.

Bell, Millicent. *Meaning in Henry James*. Cambridge: Harvard University Press, 1991.

Cohen, Paula Marantz. "Freud's *Dora* and James's *Turn of the Screw:* Two Treatments of the Female 'Case,' " *Criticism* 28 (1986), 73–87.

DeKoven, Marianne. "A Different Story: 'The Yellow Wallpaper' and *The Turn of the Screw*," in *Rich and Strange: Gender, History, Modernism*. Princeton: Princeton University Press, 1991, pp. 38–63.

Eakin, Paul John. *The New England Girl: Cultural Ideals in Hawthorne, Stowe, Howells, and James*. Athens, Ga.: University of Georgia Press, 1976.

Felman, Shoshana. "Turning the Screw of Interpretation," *Yale French Studies* 55–56 (1977), 95–207.

Gard, Roger, ed. *Henry James: The Critical Heritage*. New York: Barnes & Noble, 1968.

Halttunen, Karen. " 'Through the Cracked and Fragmented Self': William James and *The Turn of the Screw*," *American Quarterly* 40 (1988), 472–89.

Lukacher, Ned. " 'Hanging Fire': The Primal Scene of *The Turn of the Screw*," in *Henry James's Daisy Miller, The Turn of the Screw, and Other Tales*. Ed. Harold Bloom. New York: Chelsea House, 1987, pp. 117–32.

Maves, Carl. *Sensuous Pessimism: Italy in the Work of Henry James*. Bloomington: Indiana University Press, 1973.

Rowe, John Carlos. *Theoretical Dimensions of Henry James*. Madison: University of Wisconsin Press, 1984.

Samuels, Charles Thomas. *The Ambiguity of Henry James*. Urbana: University of Illinois Press, 1971.

Shine, Muriel. *The Fictional Children of Henry James*. Chapel Hill: University of North Carolina Press, 1969.

Wardley, Lynn. "Reassembling Daisy Miller," *American Literary History* 3 (1991), 232–53.